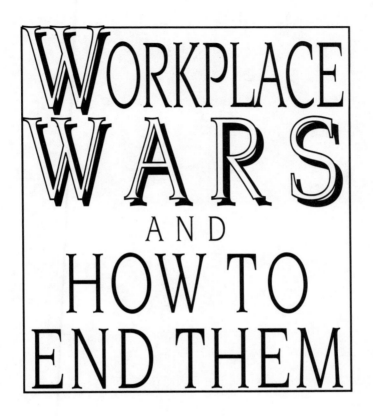

WORKPLACE WARS
AND
HOW TO END THEM

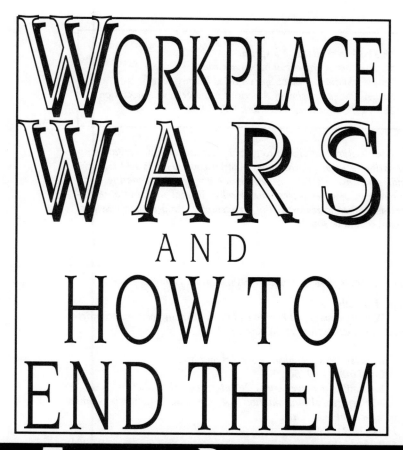

WORKPLACE WARS AND HOW TO END THEM

TURNING PERSONAL CONFLICTS INTO PRODUCTIVE TEAMWORK

KENNETH KAYE

amacom

American Management Association

New York • Atlanta • Boston • Chicago • Kansas City • San Francisco • Washington, D.C.
Brussels • Mexico City • Tokyo • Toronto

Library of Congress Cataloging-in-Publication Data

Kaye, Kenneth.
    Workplace wars and how to end them : turning personal conflicts into productive teamwork / Kenneth Kaye.
        p.   cm.
    Includes bibliographical references and index.
    ISBN 0-8144-0215-1
    1. Conflict management.   2. Interpersonal conflict.
3. Interpersonal confrontation.   4. Communication in personnel management.   I. Title.
    HD42.K39   1994
    650.13 — dc20   94-204
                                                                     CIP

Printing number

10   9   8   7   6   5   4   3   2   1

*For
my
family*

Contents

Acknowledgments

This work is most indebted to the training programs at the Family Institute of Chicago, an affiliate of Northwestern University. Many of these techniques were developed there by Professor William Pinsof for problem-centered therapy with family systems. I have adapted them for application to other kinds of organizational conflict.

I am grateful, too, to the many clients over a ten-year period who let me try to help them as systematically as I could. They were more than just the subjects on whom I foisted these various plans, strategies, exercises, and techniques; they were also brainstormers, innovators, and informants about other experiences with successful and unsuccessful attempts at conflict resolution.

Participants in my professional seminars, including attorneys, accountants, organizational consultants, and human resources managers, allowed me to try different ways of presenting the book's contents, whose organization evolved into the "system" of Plan A, Plan B, and so forth. As the new textbook for my conflict resolution training workshops, this book reflects the thoughtful feedback of those past attendees.

Thanks to my assistant, Katharine Francis, for thorough and wise suggestions on the writing style. Finally, I am most appreciative of the encouragement and editorial problem-solving talents of Adrienne Hickey at AMACOM Books and Jacqueline Laks Gorman.

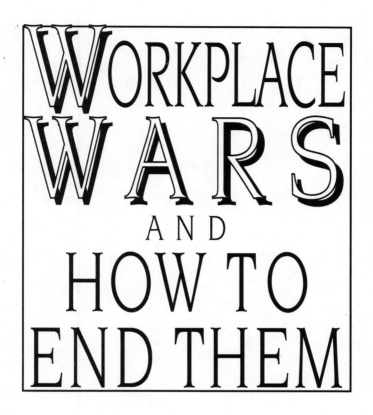

WORKPLACE WARS
AND
HOW TO
END THEM

1

"There They Go Again"

No organization is so excellent, no team so unified, no business so successful that it is immune to internal conflict. Misunderstandings arise. Personalities clash. Petty irritations mount. If no one stands up to the natural course of human emotions, bitter infighting and backstabbing erupt. People battle openly for turf or refuse to communicate at all. In the worst cases, mutual distrust can deteriorate to verbal abuse or even a fistfight, like the widely publicized brawl among the four principal family heirs of U-Haul corporation at that public company's annual meeting. Less dramatic but no less destructive are the issues that stay underground, manifested only in poor teamwork. "We don't have real conflict," one CEO said, "but I can't get our people to work together." That *is* real conflict.

Where Would We Be Without Conflict?

It is not the aim of this book to avoid, eliminate, or even minimize organizational conflict. That would be as undesirable as it is impossible. Instead, this book will help you build the kind of teamwork that *acknowledges* conflict sooner rather than later, *works it out* straightforwardly and constructively, and *uses it* as opportunity for change. Teamwork doesn't mean sitting around together in harmony. It means moving forward together: turning differences into strengths, improving group communications and problem-solving skills, and adapting the whole organization to meet its goals more effectively in a changing world.

The *Wall Street Journal* had this to say about Microsoft Corporation's race to build NT, a new operating system for personal computers:

> Immense stakes are riding on NT. But the making of NT also illustrates how innovation, in an age of technological complexity, usually requires dogged system-building and an ability to hold large teams together while allowing—even cultivating—conflict. Conflict lies at the core of innovation . . . says Emanuel R. Piore, a former chief scientist for International Business Machines Corp. "When there's no conflict, a lab is no good."[1]

Conflict means the opportunity to learn. It forces creativity. If necessity is the mother of invention, conflict is its father. When Smith's proposal antagonizes Jones or fails to address a problem from Jones's point of view, both Smith and Jones take it back to their drawing boards. They are forced to be creative, together, to achieve their separate aims without causing mutual problems and misperceptions.

Two heads are better than one only if they contain different opinions.

Conflict is also opportunity for personal growth. When Smith manages to work things out with Jones, she learns something she can apply in other situations as well. Each such experience contributes to her seeing herself as an effective person. Furthermore, it actually makes her more effective, as she anticipates other people's needs.

It really isn't the conflict itself but the opportunity to *resolve* conflict that helps to develop talent in all members of the organization. If you relieve them of distracting anger and frustration, you remove the obstacles they were throwing in the paths of one another's work, thus empowering them to develop their abilities to the fullest extent.

Finally, conflict is an opportunity for selection. Let's not deny the competitive aspect of dispute resolution. It isn't always win/win, even when the process is constructive. The argument may lead to decisions that cause factories or departments to cease operations or individual employees to lose their jobs. But that isn't bad for the organization (it isn't always bad for the individuals, either), so long as we have confidence that our decision-making processes are leading to the right cuts. What is bad is to lose good people because they're fed up with an atmosphere of bullying, shouting, backstabbing, and other insults to their self-esteem.

Conflict is neither good nor bad. Properly managed, it is absolutely vital. What would your organization be like with no conflict? It would survive, probably for years, but comatose: brain dead. Its members wouldn't develop as individuals or as a team. Every group needs problems to face and disagreements to resolve.

However, some conflicts are better than others.

You are director of human resources for an advertising agency. Its creative writers and artists look contemptuously at the account executives, treating their input as stupid meddling. The account side has ample opportunity to retaliate by criticizing the creative work and failing to show enthusiasm for it in the presence of clients. Accusations of sexual discrimination and harassment exacerbate the lack of teamwork. Your boss, the agency's president, doesn't see how she has contributed to the problem.

The tension between creativity and responsiveness to the client's needs is a central fact in the advertising industry, and the success of an agency (as in many other businesses) depends upon communication between people of completely different temperaments and talents. Unfortunately, the agency described here is gaining none of the benefits of those differences because the conflict has escalated so far. No one who works for that agency feels any longer that "conflict is opportunity."

Open, productive argument is wonderful, but conflict seething below the surface, rage boiling over destructively, chronic patterns of mutual finger-pointing, or "passive-aggressive" non-cooperation are costly, sometimes devastating, and always painful to behold.

> If we manage conflict constructively, we harness its energy for creativity and development.

It's up to us whether we manage the inevitable conflict in our organizations constructively or just complain bitterly and helplessly while the situation worsens—the unhappiness festers, the conflict escalates, the enterprise's functioning disintegrates, and the best and brightest flee to more supportive working environments.

This book is a manual for unlocking the energy of good people who are locked in combat.

The Cost of Unresolved Conflict

When the conflicting parties belong to the same group, family, or business organization, the price of warfare is almost always greater than either side can hope to gain. Consider the many costs that can result from failure to resolve conflict within your company:

Lost productivity:	Lack of team initiatives
	Employees failing to facilitate each other's work
	Time wasted by employees wrangling with each other, talking to sympathizers, and brooding about problems
Direct costs:	Capital plant and equipment carelessly treated, vandalized, stolen
	Overpayments due to lack of diligence and poor discussion of purchasing or hiring decisions
	Cash crisis (possible bankruptcy or sale) due to failure to plan
Perception costs:	Lost customers through discourtesy or poor service

	Reduced attractiveness of company to investors
	Reduced credibility to bankers
Legal costs:	Prolonged deliberation over succession, estate, restructuring plans, etc.
	Prolonged debates while professional advisors' clocks are running
	Advice on dealing with threats of litigation
	Litigation itself (plaintiff and/or defense)
Costs of not having the best people in the right jobs:	Replacing employees who leave due to conflict
	Keeping poorer employees when better ones can't be hired because of conflict
	Unnecessary perks, cars, and excessive compensation to nonperforming family members on payroll (many family-run businesses pay a high price for obvious, and unsuccessful, attempts to "avoid" conflict in this way)
	Private compensation by owner to make things "fair" to family members not employed in the business
	Bad investment decisions
	Cost of delay on good decisions

Regardless of whether you are one of the combatants, their supervisor, or an outsider charged with helping them improve their relationship, you can't afford to prolong a situation that isn't going to improve.

On the other hand, you don't want to waste human potential by giving up on people (firing them, for example) if their problems could have been solved.

Let me not mislead you. No one can resolve every interpersonal conflict amicably. Not every difficult associate can become a great teammate. The first question is whether a problem

> You don't want to waste time and money prolonging a situation that isn't going to get better. But you don't want to lose good people whose problems could have been solved.

can be resolved without terminating the relationship. Like paramedics at a disaster scene, you need to do a kind of triage, choosing whether to stanch the bleeding or reset bones or disinfect or apply the verbal equivalents of analgesics or tranquilizers. In some cases, you will remove life support systems altogether.

Is This Book for You?

You may be a manager whose formal responsibilities include team building and communications, an organizational consultant who regularly takes on such assignments, or just an individual caught up in such a conflict yourself. You may have been asked to help two or more coworkers resolve a feud or turf war just because you have a reputation for fairness, patience, and diplomacy.

Perhaps no one assigned you this responsibility, but you are fed up with the unproductive conflict among your colleagues. Their tension and distrust impedes your work, makes your life unpleasant, and endangers the health of the business. You hope to persuade them to let you help.

The ideas and methods discussed here apply equally whether you are a party to the conflict or a third party trying to be helpful.

How do you know if the conflict you have in mind is the kind this book addresses? It is if two conditions are true: First, the conflicting parties need to restore (or create for the first time) a good relationship. A settlement that leaves them never speaking to one another again, like the Montagues and the Capulets, won't be satisfactory. This is obviously true when the parties are blood relatives or in-laws in a family business; but it's just as true if they are unrelated fellow members of an organization that doesn't want to lose any of them.

In addition, the conflict isn't just about dollars or other resources. Even if it began over money, it has become personal and emotional. You can use this system when the parties claim their dispute is about money but it really isn't. You can use it when they claim it isn't about money but it really is. We won't discuss labor negotiations and grievance arbitrations, but after a labor conflict is "settled" and people are back at work together, their residual resentments and distrust may need some of the approaches in this book. You won't need this system if all parties would be satisfied with a purely financial settlement.

Building Better Relations

Why a book on only this type of conflict—managing disputes *within* organizations? What difference does it make whether the parties are members of the same organization or have little to do with each other? Aren't the methods for settling disputes pretty much the same?

Absolutely not, which is why this book needed to be written. But the key in determining which type of conflict you are dealing with isn't whether the disputing parties are strangers, friends, neighbors, or associates beforehand. It is *what they intend to be afterward.*

Suppose a truck plows into your car, causing serious financial damage. The moment that happens, you have a relationship with the owner of the truck. Settling the dispute consists of bringing that relationship to a conclusion and going your separate ways.

Now consider a different kind of collision. Your business partner makes a large purchase of inventory that conflicts with your intention to change your product line. Ending the relationship is only one possible, drastic way to settle such a dispute. You might elect it as a last resort, but only if more constructive efforts fail. You would prefer to achieve confluence of the partners' visions and actions.

You wouldn't call a divorce attorney if you wanted to save your marriage. Don't call the author of this book if you want to sue the pants off somebody. Those different aims require two completely different kinds of expertise. However, the skills required for turning conflict into confluence are much the same whether it is a matter between small-business owners, managers of a huge corporation, or a family feud. (The issues and the personalities will be different, but you'll use many of the same methods to resolve them.)

Although people's attempts to rid themselves of one another earn more headlines, most of life's conflicts are not of the divorcing kind. Everyday life consists of head butting between people who need one another's cooperation, not obliteration. The last thing they want in the way of resolution is to settle on some dollar figure and walk away from their relationship. Whether their quarrel is mainly economic or emotional (or both), the parties cannot simply settle the matter and go their separate ways, never to see each other again. They need to make it better.

Conflict Resolution Within Groups vs. Between Parties

I mentioned two conditions that will tell you when you need this book. Once you decide you do, three important features distinguish conflict resolution within groups from the settlement of disputes between separate parties. These features are true whether the conflict involves only a couple of people or a whole organization and whether that organization is large or small.

First, *within-group conflict is always personal and emotional,* even if it begins with impersonal issues. We all carry baggage from our childhoods and from our journeys through life, and the frustrated, resentful members of any group trapped in conflict cannot help dumping or spilling some of that baggage into their joint laundry pile. Thus their anger, hurt, distrust, envy, or fear toward those they have to work with can be as intense as similar feelings toward siblings, parents, or a spouse.

Conflict resolution in a business organization doesn't require deeply analyzing the transference from individuals' personal histories into their current relationship. However, an agent of change often needs to push people beneath the superficial matters they are ostensibly fighting about to the sometimes irrational but nonetheless important issues that motivate them.

When personal animosities contradict the social pressure for group solidarity, the result is internal (intrapsychic) conflict. We feel we *should* like that person or at least get along with him or her, if only for the sake of our common enterprise—but he or she is an exceptionally inconsiderate or hostile or selfish or crazy individual, not a real member of the team. We hold on to that belief in order to rationalize our negative feelings. Once having formed the opinion that such a person is not to be trusted, we have difficulty believing evidence to the contrary. We will look for the slightest confirmation of our negative expectations of that individual; we may discount many positive subsequent encounters.

The second distinguishing feature of within-group conflicts is *their quality of "here we go again."* They tend to recur in a predictable cycle from intolerable clash to uneasy truce and back again. A wise change agent can chart this chronic pattern and plan how to interrupt the pattern, divert it, and introduce more adaptive ways of dealing with issues.

Third, the most important thing about all the conflicts we shall address is the goal I mentioned previously, *confluence:* to get the parties moving along the same path, toward common aims, by mutual support and teamwork.

The Systematic Approach

You already possess some peacemaking skills, acquired either by formal training or just through daily life. For example, you may be good at active listening, the habit of checking to be sure you understand others' positions and they understand yours. This book will add to your repertoire of techniques, but more importantly, it will organize your conflict resolution methods systematically. It presents a *system* for approaching any conflict and keeping your work on a productive track.

The system actually involves a sequence of approaches: Plan A, Plan B, Plan C, Plan D, and Plan E. The next five chapters explain those plans one by one. The purpose of each plan (and thus of chapters 2 through 6) is either to help the group reframe a particular conflict to a problem they can solve as a team or to lay the groundwork for taking the conflict on to the next plan.

Plan A: *Look for Shared Goals and Win/Win Solutions*

Chapter 2 discusses the approach you'll begin with and keep returning to: focusing attention on the shared goals and the parties' compatible goals. A conflict becomes merely a problem when the whole group can brainstorm together and act cooperatively to tackle it. It will still require creativity, coordination, feedback, and other aspects of teamwork. But from the point of view of this book, a conflict is no longer a conflict when the group is addressing problems together.

Techniques used in Plan A are active listening (listening well yourself and coaching others to do so), goal sorting, and encouraging candor about the feelings and concerns behind people's goals.

Plan B: *Clarify, Sort, and Value Differences*

Chapter 3 takes up those expressed goals, concerns, and perceptions that are not shared by all the parties. Some are based on misunderstandings, which you can clear up. Some are differences in point of view—from personal communication styles to cultural and occupational mind-sets. Your job is to turn those point of view (POV) differences into strengths of the team or of the whole organization, instead of sources of conflict. Plan B also sorts out issues resulting from individual personality problems, mental health problems, or unacceptable bias.

As former differences vanish or become less important, this approach can lead you back to Plan A. On the other hand, it can also clarify what each person needs to change (Plan C) if they are to work as a team.

Do you have to psychoanalyze the group or its individual personalities before they can change their ways of interacting? No. Analyzing personalities has its value but also its limits.

Psychological testing or counseling can offer some insights, which people with the right attitudes and openness may be able to use constructively. However, insights without action plans are unlikely to work any magic.

Plan C: Gain Commitment to Change

In Chapter 4 you will learn some techniques for shifting people (including yourself, if you are part of the problem) away from mutual blaming and on to a commitment to change their own behavior.

The words *change* and *resist* are like heads and tails of the same coin—or Yin and Yang. The more change occurs or is proposed, the more resistance will be encountered. Therefore getting people to accept change may require reassuring them in various ways that the needed changes are really very small, always under their own control, and that they aren't directed by others but by motives they themselves have expressed.

Armed with a greater willingness to change their attitudes and behavior, the group then goes back to Plans A and B. Often that is enough to break their logjam. If not, you are ready with Plan D.

Plan D: Analyze the Recurring Cycle

Suppose the dispute doesn't go away. It keeps rearing its ugly head, a tragic waste of human resources. Fortunately, the repetitive patterns in these conflicts are sometimes what enable us to resolve them. We can analyze those predictable patterns, block them, and reinforce the group's constructive patterns instead. Chapter 5 shows how to use what you can readily observe about a particular interpersonal conflict not only to help stop that familiar cycle but also to produce significant, constructive, sustainable change in the whole system's dynamics.

Such insights can shake up the system by provoking more-thoughtful behavior, giving everyone reason to stop and reflect on their habitual responses. However, as I've said, organizational change isn't likely to happen just because someone has a glimmer of perception into the "prehistoric" or unconscious dynamics that shape group behavior. Ultimately, organizational change requires strategies and tools that are designed to lead to actions more than insights.

> Action plans may work even if they aren't based on profound insight about underlying psychodynamics. Without action plans, insights (no matter how profound) aren't likely to work any magic.

Plan E: Unilaterally Demonstrate Change

Plans B or C or D may lead you—or one of the parties—to conclude that the other people in the conflict are not going to change. This still leaves one approach to be tried before giving up on the relationship altogether: unilateral change. Changes in one person can give everyone else something different to respond to.

Chapter 6 shows how to minimize the risk of unilateral "disarmament" and how to maximize its positive impact.

The Flow of the System

The system presented in this book is so straightforward that we can display it in a flowchart, shown in Figure 1-1. As indicated, when people have a disagreement, there are only two acceptable resolutions:

1. Happily *celebrate your success* when the team attacks the problem together, so it is no longer a conflict; or
2. Regrettably *cut your losses* by terminating relationships.

Although the latter possibility may mean a failure of one's hopes, I consider it a successful resolution as compared to hopelessly prolonging the battle. That is why the flowchart repeatedly returns to the decision point labeled "Still worth trying?" If Plan A isn't effective, we make a judgment whether it is worth trying Plan B. If that doesn't work, we again make a

Figure 1-1. Flowchart of systematic conflict resolution.

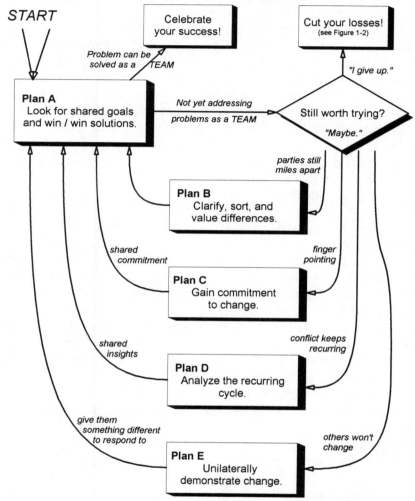

judgment whether to try Plan C, and so on. There are no rules about rigidly stepping through the plans, but in general one always keeps in sight the objective of returning to Plan A and reframing the "conflict" as just a "joint problem."

This logic guarantees resolution by the minimum means necessary. Provided, of course, that you might accept as a resolution something like "the individual isn't going to change—

fire her" or "quit your job—you've done everything you can, and the organization won't change."

That is why the question of when and how to "give up" figures as prominently in Figure 1-1 as "celebrate your success." Figure 1-2 expands the top of the flowchart. It is a question of whether to keep looking for the win/win solution or to try for win/lose (and avoid being one of the losers). If your own goals don't include destroying the other party (yet), then you'll keep trying. Go back to Plan A, B, C, D, or E. Even if you would love to do away with the other party but you're not willing to risk much damage to yourself, then, too, you should return to the flowchart and keep trying.

You can always bail out later.

Suppose you are the creative services director at the advertising agency described earlier. Concerned about the backbiting, morale problems, and unproductive internal competition, you pressed the president to address the problem. You have supported the human resources people, welcomed the program they initiated, and have done everything you could to improve communications from your side of the organization. Increasingly, however, it becomes clear that the head of account services refuses to work with you no matter what you say or do. He denies the possibility that he or his people are in any way responsible for any of the problems. Worse, for the president to see how wrong that view is, she would have to acknowledge that her own management style has not worked—an idea to which she shows no sign of being open. You can work with her, but not with your sworn enemy in charge of account services. Either he goes or you go.

If you find that the other party is looking for blood and isn't going to be satisfied with a resolution in which everyone wins, then you can head for the upper right corner of the chart, "Cut your losses." Ask yourself how much damage you are willing to sustain (the loss of your own job, a failure to meet department goals, or a further decline in morale) in the battle to destroy the other. If the answer is "much," like a kamikaze pilot or the hero who only regrets that he has but one life to give for his country, then you don't need my help.

Figure 1-2. The hope of win/win—or the risk of lose/lose?

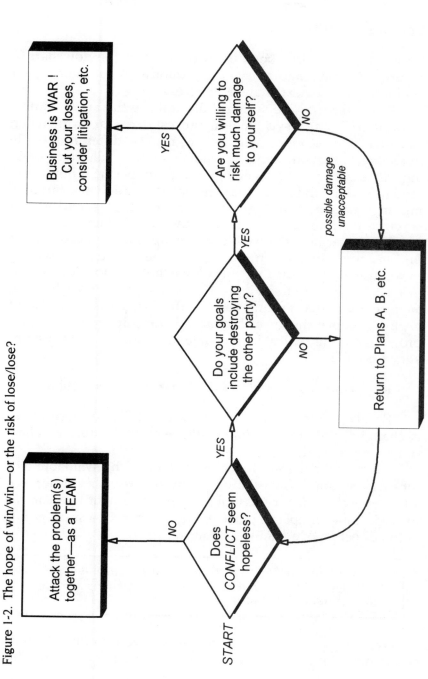

Science or Art?

I have organized this book to correspond to the flowchart in Figure 1-1. Each chapter lays the groundwork for taking your conflict on to the next chapter, if necessary.

Does this maplike system fully capture the art of conflict resolution? Many psychological processes are at work when consultants or leaders help people resolve differences—role modeling, imitation, bonding, transference, equilibrium seeking, ritualization. As psychology is a primitive art, I don't pretend to understand fully what I myself do for a living. But having my map in mind gives me a sense of security and empowerment to venture a little farther into the forest.

No matter how the conflict blows up, I know I can at least find my way home again. This makes me a little more willing to venture down paths that may or may not lead to a resolution.

That is how to use Figure 1-1 as well as the flowcharts in later chapters that expand each of the five plans. They don't begin to reduce the art of human relationships to a computer program but they will at least enable the reader to be as systematic as possible.

Incorporating This System Into the Organizational Culture

Resolving a conflict is always worthwhile; but even better is changing the organizational culture so that future conflicts resolve more easily.

Chapter 7 suggests that this system is an invaluable tool for every organizational change agent to have in his or her tool kit. It is both a diagnostic tool and an instrument that can, in the right time and place, push an organization or a small group in the direction of a teamwork culture.

> We won't be satisfied to resolve the current problem. We need significant, constructive, sustainable change in the whole system's dynamics.

Whenever you try to help people resolve a conflict, the outcome might be rated along a kind of ladder (Figure 1-3). The

Figure 1-3. Hierarchy of team-building outcomes.

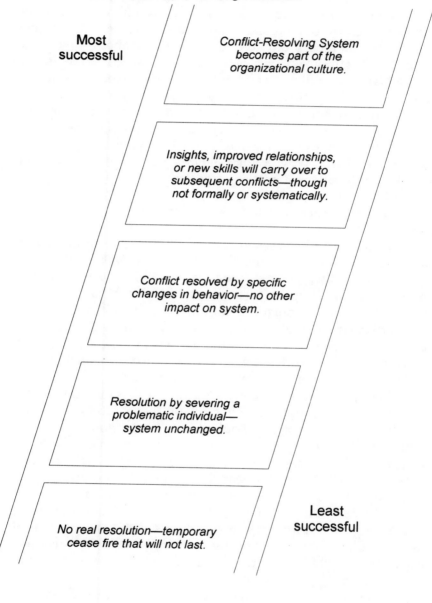

Most successful

Conflict-Resolving System becomes part of the organizational culture.

Insights, improved relationships, or new skills will carry over to subsequent conflicts—though not formally or systematically.

Conflict resolved by specific changes in behavior—no other impact on system.

Resolution by severing a problematic individual— system unchanged.

Least successful

No real resolution—temporary cease fire that will not last.

highest aspiration you, as an agent of change, might set your sights on is to institutionalize this entire system of conflict resolution within your organization's culture so that it becomes part of the members' day-to-day expectations about their teamwork. At that point, I suggest giving it a name such as [Company Name] Conflict-Resolving System and celebrating it as a sustainable competitive advantage for your organization.

In the experience of my clients, the transformation to a Conflict-Resolving System (CRS) occurs only when the culture is ripe for it in the first place and when your assignment is broadly defined. It won't happen merely as a felicitous byproduct of resolving a particular dispute.

Conflict Management and Team Building

Team building has several facets. One facet reflects the personal qualities and management style of the *leaders* of the organization as a whole and of the teams within it. Another facet is *structural:* finding the most productive functional units, job descriptions, and reporting relationships. Then comes the *personnel* department: getting the best people in the right jobs with effective incentives. And finally, under the heading *culture,* team building includes expectations about appropriate attitudes and modes of behavior in this organization.

The task of resolving conflicts and maintaining effective internal communications touches all of those facets. In other words, the subject of this book is only a component of team building. Yet it is the sine qua non: without which, nothing. When you have problems with turf boundaries, job descriptions, or reporting relationships, you need to resolve conflict. When compensation schemes are inconsistent or unfair, when career paths clash with changes in the organization's needs, when longtime employees' expectations differ from those of new recruits, conflict has to be resolved. And when leaders' expectations collide with the organization's long-standing culture, conflict has to be resolved.

Unfortunately, this sine qua non is the least developed area of knowledge among all those aspects of team building. Your library contains many more titles about leadership, structure, personnel, and culture than it contains about resolving conflict. Until now, conflict resolution consisted of a grab bag of primitive tools. CRS puts those tools together systematically for the benefit of the whole team-building endeavor.

Exercises vs. a Team-Building Strategy

You will find two differences here from other material you may have read about resolving conflict or improving confluence within organizations.

First, the book contains no artificial exercises to change attitudes or improve communications. I regard such exercises as overused and overrated. People are stimulated by engaging in them but don't consistently transfer enough back to their working lives to justify the time and expense. It can be more efficient as well as more effective to use the actual conflicts your people are struggling with as the material for your team-building sessions.

The second difference is that this material is more than just a list of approaches you can try. The flowchart *guarantees* resolution, one way or another. As you keep moving through the plans, you will keep returning to the questions in Figure 1-2. Either you will get people tackling their problems together or you will redefine their relationships. The system won't let you stagnate in prolonged, unresolved complaining and finger pointing.

In short, you don't have to be stymied by personal conflict in your organization. Nor do you have to choose whether to concentrate on the present crisis or to build better functioning teams for the future. You should always be doing both. When faced straightforwardly, your conflict is an opportunity to build teamwork, enhance productivity, and achieve personal growth all at the same time.

Who Is in Charge of Conflict Resolution?

One word of advice before you proceed. This field is not for the timid. The role of confluence facilitator demands that you assert control over the process, not over the solution. The disputants are going to solve their problem; you aren't. But they need you to be active and in control of the process.

You cannot put only your toe in these turbulent waters or wade in only up to your ankles. To help people who are drowning, you must be prepared to swim.

> All your actions as a mediator are also demonstrations of good communication.

Disputants can scream and yell at one another without your help. They can trade accusations, fail to respond to one another's concerns, avoid the real issues, deny responsibility, and resist change, all without your help. You are there to make a difference! Take responsibility for maintaining a civil dialogue throughout all the following approaches. *Controlling* the process accomplishes three things at the same time. It allows you to work on the problem, obviously. But it also provides a model, through your own behavior, of how to maintain appropriate discourse. And it gives people hope that you really can help them.

You will experience change in yourself concurrently with changes in the people you help to work more effectively together. As you gain confidence, you will find it easier to inspire confidence in them. As they take the risks you encourage them to take, their trust in you will in turn make you more confident.

Remember that you are not making sick people healthy. The people you can help to change are already healthy, possessing strengths as individuals as well as natural instincts for collaboration. All you have to do is listen; join with the hopeful, constructive aspects of all sides of a dispute; and reflect back their optimism rather than their fears.

Plunge in!

Note

1. "Agony and Ecstasy of 200 Code Writers Beget Windows NT," *Wall Street Journal*, May 26, 1993, p. 1.

2

Plan A: Look for Shared Goals and Win/Win Solutions

Conflict means opportunity. It gives us reasons not to go on doing the same old things and thinking in the same old ways. Whenever conflict kicks us in the head, it creates an opportunity to exceed our own expectations.

Marvin ran the concrete contracting subsidiary of a large construction company. At 62, he had already groomed an ambitious young salesman, Ted, to take over his job if necessary. Marvin wanted to continue running it so long as his health (which was excellent) permitted. He and Ted clashed frequently—for example, over Ted's desire to streamline the office or to price more aggressively. Each time, Marvin asked himself if they were really arguing about the issue of the moment or if there just wasn't room for both of them in the company. Ted began to hint, then to say outright, that he wouldn't stay if he didn't get more responsibility.

Marvin took seriously his responsibility to the owners to nurture his successor. Instead of letting the conflict drive Ted away, the two men convinced the corporate owner to let them invest in some equipment and training for custom architectural forming. That specialized service soon became profitable, justifying Marvin's full-time involvement while Ted took charge of the core business.

Had it not been for the conflict between the veteran manager and his protégé, they wouldn't have felt the pressure to take on the new venture. The company would have missed the chance to develop it before their old market, high-rise construction, dried up.

However, it wasn't the conflict itself that brought about this result. It was *the fact that Marvin and Ted reframed their issue in terms of a common goal* (to make the business complex, challenging, and profitable enough for both of them). Instead of disputing their conflicting opinions about when Marvin should retire, they framed a problem they could attack together—win/win. That is Plan A.

How to Encourage Good Disputes

It must not be our goal to prevent conflict or discourage disputes. Our goal is to encourage *good* disputes. We want people to disagree with one another freely, constructively, not always pleasantly or kindly but always respecting the legitimacy of other points of view and the value of the other person. How do some organizations do that?

Organizations that have implemented a Conflict-Resolving System (CRS):

- ❑ Focus on common goals
- ❑ Don't squelch differences
- ❑ Don't run away from emotions
- ❑ Don't tolerate the destructive, catastrophic, or wasteful kinds of disputes

These principles apply to every stage of the process, but because they begin with Plan A, we will say something here about all four principles.

Focus on Common Goals and Compatible Individual Goals

Good communication doesn't create commonality of purpose. Quite the reverse: Keeping group members focused upon their shared mission and vision makes it much easier for them to communicate so as to resolve differences productively. Figure 2-1 shows how Plan A proceeds through three steps. First is mutual interviewing. Use active listening and "I" statements to compare what both sides really want. Second, clarify the meaningful, positive goals (setting aside the red herrings, exaggerated threats, gratuitous insults, and all other digressions from constructive collaboration). Third, prioritize the most important objectives, giving weight to those that are most shared. If you have nothing but incompatible purposes, Plan A will make that fact evident.

When you get to Plan B, you'll see how some supposedly incompatible goals can be reframed as valuable diverse points of view. The option will still exist to encourage "warfare" or power-based solutions (as shown in Figure 1-2) such as litigation, termination of the relationship, or even physical violence if you choose. But a better first step is to focus on the team's

Figure 2-1. Plan A: Look for shared goals.

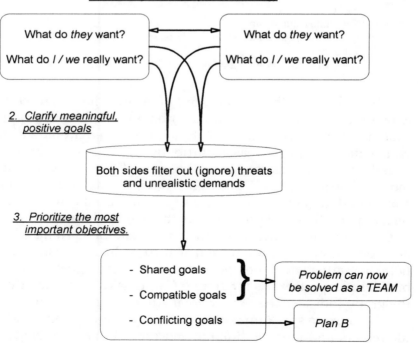

common or compatible goals (the interest-based approach) and to tackle, as a team, any problems that obstruct those purposes.

Let's see how a simple goal-sorting procedure, too often neglected, can help set aside trivial differences and create a problem-solving attitude. Imagine that you've been asked to help a group of managers address their differences constructively. Instead of functioning as a team, they have been depleting their energies, time, and the morale of others in the company with petty squabbles and power struggles. (For purposes of this illustration, the individuals' titles and types of responsibility aren't important.)

Meeting with the principal people who have problems with one another, you begin by asking everyone to spell out all the goals they can think of that might be relevant either to what caused the conflict, what's obstructing its solution, or why it must be resolved. You are going to construct a list. You ask Anne, one of the managers, to begin. Here is her list:

Person	Goal
Anne	End male chauvinism.
	I want Bob's office moved off this floor, or better yet, out of the building.
	Get Carl to take more initiative.

You ask the other participants if Anne's items are clear enough, and they indicate that the first one needs much clarification. Anne revises it: "Create a working environment in which the women's ideas, contributions, etc., are acknowledged and valued as readily as the men's." Her second item, moving Bob's office, is clear as a bell but is not really a goal. It's a proposed method for achieving a goal—reduced conflict with Bob, apparently—and probably not the best method. Nevertheless, leave it on the list. After the first round of learning what everyone thinks they want, you will come back to Anne and help her articulate more positive, longer-term goals with a broader perspective. As for getting Carl to take more initiative, the group indicates they know what Anne means by that.

The next to speak up is Bob. He wisely ignores Anne's hostile remark and raises a different concern. "I think the biggest problem for me, the only problem our group has right now, is that Susan has one foot out the door."

"Is that a goal?" the leader asks, "or is it a perception?" Bob restates it, and a couple of others assent to this goal:

Person	Goal
Bob, Anne, SuLing	Find out whether Susan has one foot out the door, or what?

The mutual interviewing proceeds until everyone has some understanding of what they all hope for as a resolution. You facilitate clarifications of all their positions and concerns, but selectively so—focusing on the positive goals. For example, you get Anne to state the real goals beyond her earlier remarks. After half an hour, the list now reads:

Person	Goal
Anne	Create a working environment in which the women's ideas, contributions, etc., are acknowledged and valued as readily as the men's. End Bob's personal animosity toward me. Get Carl to take more initiative.
Bob, Anne, SuLing	Find out whether Susan has one foot out the door, or what?
Bob	End Anne's perception of me as enemy.
Doug	Ditto.
Bob, Helen, Susan, Carl, SuLing	Get engineers to understand marketing perspective better, and vice versa. Reduce power struggle between Doug and Anne.
Carl	End Anne's paranoia. Stop Doug's usurping authority.

Now you prioritize the whole list as suggested in Figure 2-1, dividing it into shared goals, compatible goals, and conflicting goals. (Remember that in Plan A, shared goals are your first priority.) This entails further discussion, in the course of which consensus emerges. The most important goal is then clarified more specifically:

Shared goals:	Get engineers to understand marketing perspective better, and vice versa.
	Why? So we're designing for the market and marketing what we can make best.

Reducing the power struggle between Doug and Anne (the group decides) is compatible with their number-one goal. So is ending the animosity between Anne and Bob. Those goals stay on the agenda for Plan A.

Compatible goals:	Reduce power struggle between Doug and Anne.
	End personal animosity between Anne and Bob.

All other items—the apparently conflicting goals—go to the bottom of the list, to be saved for Plan B.

Conflicting goals:	Anne: Create a working environment in which the women's ideas, contributions, etc., are acknowledged and valued as readily as the men's.
	Anne: Get Carl to take more initiative.
	Bob, Anne, SuLing: Find out whether Susan has one foot out the door, or what?
	Carl: End Anne's paranoia.
	Carl: Stop Doug's usurping authority.

Not everyone agrees the organization is sexist or that Carl should take more initiative. For now (Plan A), group members will set aside all those individual differences and brainstorm about how to achieve their common goals.

Don't Squelch Differences

We have just covered the first of four characteristics of a good problem-solving culture. The second characteristic, that of not squelching differences, also begins with Plan A, although it becomes more central in Plan B.

The idea is to acknowledge differences without trying to eliminate them. You focus on the goals you might share without denying that you'll probably have to work out other, incompatible goals eventually. Plan A is merely your first step to establish a constructive win/win approach.

People who are averse to conflict frequently conciliate prematurely. They don't explore or even air their differences with one another; in other words, they have no alternatives to Plan A. This can unfortunately become a characteristic of the group's culture, a norm of avoiding disagreement. Such groups, where conflict is taboo, may turn out to be more conflicted in the long run than those whose cultures support open dissent. For the squelched differences don't go away, they just go underground. Eventually they erupt in exaggerated form. When that happens, the conflicting positions are misunderstood and lead to overreactions. Inevitably, the differences appear to be much more refractory than they really are.

A pot with the lid on comes to a boil faster—and boils over.

Who are the worst at avoiding arguments and squelching differences? Bosses or senior coworkers who can't tolerate a challenge to their own opinion. More successful leaders are comfortable with and reward people who question them and who even, at times, strongly argue against the leaders' most cherished assumptions. You need to be that kind of leader if you want teamwork among your employees.

From the employees' point of view, conflict is troublesome to the degree that it clashes with *either* their own cultural and personal comfort levels *or* their company's culture. A person who is accustomed to airing and resolving interpersonal conflicts is likely to be as distressed in a culture that suppresses dissent as people with the opposite sort of experience would be in a culture that encourages dissent.

Don't Run Away From Emotions

The third characteristic of effective problem-solving organizations follows directly from the second: Don't squelch differences *and* don't squelch emotions.

Motorola is an example of a company whose culture encourages dissent and heated emotions. It does not consider courtesy a virtue if engineers or managers withhold criticism of anyone's ideas, within their own departments or across units. One human resources manager explained to me, "We're like a family that encourages sibling rivalry among its 100,000 children." She referred to the rivalry among the company's dozen divisions and between competing research and development ideas. The company's winning philosophy is that they can't be competitive on the playing field without high emotion on the practice field and in the locker room as well.

As former Motorola CEO George Fisher put it, "Out of conflict comes catharsis."

Motorola's leaders are apparently confident that good ideas will rise to the top so long as passionate argument is allowed. They are betting that the advocates of losing ideas, shot down internally before they get a chance to be shot down in the marketplace, will only go back to the lab and dream up something better. Their frustration won't become unproductive so long as criticisms are leveled equitably.

Focusing on common goals (Plan A) will usually make the discussion less emotional. Remember, however, that you don't really want to avoid emotions altogether, only to keep them from drowning out discourse. The fact that they are under control in Plan A is not a step toward burying them; it is an opportunity to begin to acknowledge and consider those emotions that may surface more intensely later (especially in Plans B and D). Therefore let us make some observations on the psychology of emotions.

There is bound to be *jealousy*, at times, in any competitive company. Stifling it could mean stifling the passion that drives an organization toward excellence. And jealousy is only one of many emotions associated with good as well as bad disputes.

Anger can provide the energy to fuel change. Heated debate is no threat to an organization where the process is part of the culture. Only companies where such processes are foreign run the danger of falling apart when emotions erupt.

A-N-G-R-Y spells *energy.*

Anger is really a secondary emotion. The primary feeling might be unexpressed jealousy, hurt, or fear. Someone who is jealous, for example, might jump right to anger, perhaps constructing a whole rationale for the anger based on injustice without mentioning jealousy at all.

Hurt may be the commonest emotion hiding behind anger. This is because our defenses against hurt get mobilized almost before we become conscious that someone has hurt us. We are embarrassed or frightened to be so vulnerable—or we would be, if we showed the hurt. Therefore, instead of acknowledging it (even to ourselves), we go straight to the anger it arouses. Unfortunately, expressed anger doesn't inspire those at whom it is directed to be more empathic, understanding, or helpful. Anger provokes fear. Someone who is the target of anger interprets it at the level of his autonomic nervous system, not his cerebrum. It triggers his "flight" or "fight" reaction—either one. If the latter, then his angry response prompts an even more belligerent counterresponse, and so on.

The associate who has the forthrightness to express hurt directly gains a better chance of eliciting empathic listening, if not conciliation.

The best defense is *not* a good offense.

Fear is another emotion we don't always feel comfortable acknowledging. Instead of saying, "I'm afraid . . . ," we hide behind blaming others, as if there could be no doubt of their hostile intentions. For example, the manager who is afraid of being judged expendable says, "They are looking for excuses to fire me." That way of expressing the fear has two results. It puts the control in the hands of others by labeling herself a passive, helpless victim. And it puts those others on the defensive, alienating the very people who might have helped her.

Thus there is nothing to be gained by denying the fear to oneself or hiding it from others. Acknowledging fear puts a good motive on the table for everyone to work with as they seek win/win solutions.

Sadness and *loss* are feelings with which many men are uncomfortable in business settings, probably just because they are the opposite of macho. Yet denying them doesn't fool anyone.

It is only harder for others to relate to someone who puts a stoic face on a devastating personal setback.

Henry just had a whole department taken away from him after he spent nearly a year reorganizing it. He had replaced the dead wood with some technical superstars gleaned from a national search. Upper management's decision thus wiped out the most satisfying part of his work. Part of him feels like crying, as he would if a tornado flattened his house. But Henry suppresses that feeling and goes directly to righteous indignation. It wasn't fair! (As if fairness has anything to do with such decisions.)

Wrong move. Appropriate statements of loss and sadness generate empathy and understanding; complaints about injustice and conspiracies do not. It is not a question of whether Henry is right in thinking other parties are out to get him. Even if they are, he'd be better off expressing sadness and his fear of further loss than attributing nefarious motives to them.

Guilt is almost by definition a secret emotion. Afraid to admit that we may have wronged someone, we deny responsibility and blame others—even blame the victim. Often, however, one has nothing to lose by owning responsibility for a problem. That doesn't preclude asking others to share in the responsibility for resolving it.

Finally, consider *shame*. The sense of inadequacy is one of our deepest driving feelings, yet one of the hardest to own publicly. It feels extra shameful to admit shame or embarrassment. How disarming it can be, though, if you do: Expecting to hear excuses, your coworkers hear, "I feel ashamed that I failed to meet that deadline."

Would you think less of someone who made a statement like that? Or more highly? Might you not immediately begin to list the factors beyond his or her control that led to the project's failure? You might even have more confidence in this manager's dedication and judgment when the next project comes along.

Notice something about all the emotions I have touched on here. If organizational norms discourage their expression—or if individuals instinctively suppress them—there is a human tendency to disguise these emotions behind more hostile, de-

---

When organizational norms discourage the expression of "weaknesses" such as hurt, fear, sadness, or shame, people are more likely to substitute aggressive feelings (jealousy, anger, desire for revenge) and to escalate disputes to the point where Plan A is impossible.

---

fensive attacks that only make resolution more difficult. Or, perhaps worse, one suppresses all reaction at the time when one's feelings could have been best dealt with, so they are postponed—only to resurface later, more destructively.

Don't Tolerate the Destructive, Catastrophic, or Wasteful Kinds of Disputes

Besides focusing on goals, valuing differences of opinion, and encouraging the expression of emotions, the fourth thing successful problem-solving organizations do is refuse to allow rancor to fester. Members insist on a fair fight, which means that a process of better understanding and problem solving has to become a norm of the organization: "We don't fight destructively; we fight constructively."

Although her responsibility is cost accounting, Liz has an interest in the quality of teamwork throughout the plant. So she is concerned when she hears voices raised in the office. "I told you to stay out of my shop," shouts a foreman named Harry. Liz's assistant, Chang, replies abusively. Four-letter words fly back and forth, and Chang lunges toward the older man, but a coworker restrains him.

The head of manufacturing, Liz's boss, emerges from his office and says, "Okay, Harry, you made your point. Now go back to the shop and cool off."

After Harry withdraws and Chang goes outside for a cigarette, Liz listens as their coworkers recount the fight and speculate about what led to it. Her boss has returned to a telephone call, but when she sees him hang up, she asserts herself. "I think it's important to let them clear the air," she says. "Cooling off won't solve it."

A few minutes later, both managers sit with Harry and Chang

in the otherwise empty lunchroom. "Something that could get you both so upset must be important," Liz says. "Resolving it is even more important. We need you to take turns listening to what happened from the other guy's point of view."

It doesn't happen that way, unfortunately, in most organizations. It is too tempting to hope things will blow over—and often they do. But the negative effect on morale, of the observers as well as the antagonists, is cumulative.

You won't always be able to respond so quickly as in the foregoing example, but the sooner the better (provided tempers have cooled a little). Just make it a rule: No wound is allowed to fester, no hostilities are allowed to wear on and on. Any serious personal conflict in the organization becomes priority number one. Like a married couple who pledge never to end the day angry at one another, the organization members should expect to treat any conflict as an acute minicrisis before it becomes chronic. An insincere "forget it" is never allowed to be the last word. No "business as usual" while the conflict continues to boil.

COMPANY POLICY: No one in this organization goes home for the weekend holding a grudge. If you're fighting mad, that's okay—so long as by Friday you have either resolved it with the parties concerned or set up a process that will lead to a win/win resolution.

It isn't easy to insist on continuing to talk about a conflict that has simmered down temporarily. What comes more naturally, when tension drops from 6 on the Richter scale down to a mere 2 or 3, than to breathe a sigh of relief and just put it out of mind? The hard thing is to say, "This is important," and to insist on exploring the problem when other people would just as soon back away from it.

Of course, there is value in letting fighters withdraw to their corners. They do need to cool off. But there is danger in letting them pretend to believe the fight is over when it is not.

Ideally, the cease-fire is a time for constructive, sustainable problem solving.

You may hear denial when there is a cease-fire: "It won't happen again." At the very least, get the antagonists to pledge that they will engage in heavy-duty armistice talks if and when their hostilities do resume.

The Art of Listening

Solving interpersonal problems is an ordinary, routine part of everyone's responsibility as a member of a team. That's what it means to have CRS as part of your culture. You don't want to bring in a consultant to mediate every serious dispute. You need *normative* structures that encourage debate rather than debacle. Norms are the ways people in an organization expect one another to behave. With CRS, people come to expect that interpersonal problems will be resolved. Dealing with even the most intense conflict will not be an extraordinary process; it will be understood as normal.

Figure 2-2 lists other such norms, dos and don'ts to add to the four discussed above. There is something curious about this list. All the behaviors in the left column come quite naturally to us when we interact with people we don't have close relationships with or whose favor we don't take for granted: customers, for example. You wouldn't think of calling your customer a name or accusing her of deliberately trying to confound you. Unfortunately, it seems to be one of the foibles of human nature that between family members, lovers, and in any group of individuals who work closely together and think they know each other fairly well, people begin to take one another for granted and thus neglect many of the amenities that human discourse has evolved for airing differences without debacle.

This means that most interpersonal conflict within organizations (and also within families) can be avoided entirely if people simply treat their fellow members as their most important clients. What is foremost in our minds when we talk with customers and clients? Not our differences of opinion or conflicting interests but our interest in providing the goods or services

Figure 2-2. Dos and don'ts for teamwork.

Cultural norms that encourage DEBATE	Cultural norms that encourage DEBACLE

Focus on common goals:

Institutionalize win/win procedures.	Encourage win/lose competition.
Insist on investigative clarification.	Let actions be based on assumptions or subjective impressions.
Demand "what can we do to help?"	Demand excuses. Let each feel accused or endangered.
Emphasize planning and preparation for change.	Keep 'em guessin'.

Don't squelch differences:

Create safe harbors for retreat.	Corner people until their views match.
Base promotions on performance, evaluated as objectively as possible.	Base promotions on favoritism or apparently arbitrary factors.
Label dissenting views as valued contributions.	Stress unity and loyalty to the point of suppressing dissent, complaints, and meaningful communication outside of reporting relationships.
Label expressions of discontent as important information.	

Don't run away from emotions:

Respect introspection; validate the emotional side; support therapy as a way for individuals to separate current issues from their personal unresolved conflicts.	Treat emotion as a weakness, therapy as the refuge of weaklings and psychos.

Don't tolerate destructive kinds of disputes:

Insist on face-to-face discussion.	Let each faction's members complain among themselves about "those guys."
Insist on rules of active listening.	
Insist on addressing acts, not persons.	Let them antagonize each other.

they need. If we slip into a more oppositional mode of discourse with family members or teammates, it is usually because we take the relationship and our shared goals for granted. *We skip Plan A.* We either forget about or resent the question, "What can we do to make the relationship work?"—a question that is second nature in less important relationships.

People do their most effective communicating with complete strangers. Active listening is what all of us do, for exam-

> Most breakdowns in teamwork would never happen if we remembered to treat our teammates with the basic courtesies we normally extend to customers.

ple, when we ask for or give directions. The less well we know the other person, the more we instinctively use the techniques of active listening. We do it most of all if there is a partial language barrier or a noisy channel, as was typically the case in the early days of citizens band (CB) radios. But even in an ordinary dialogue, when you are talking with a customer, you don't assume that your job is to talk and his job is to understand you. You take responsibility for ensuring that he does understand and for clarifying anything he doesn't understand: You don't blame *him* if he is confused. And you also take responsibility for *listening* and for making him *know* that you listened and understood what he wanted to say or ask. Even when you can't gratify his request, you can make him feel positive about interacting with you.

The rules of active listening are:

Rules for the Speaker

1. Must not yield the floor until (s)he feels listened to.
2. Should not ask a question until (s)he is prepared to switch roles and listen to the answer.

Rules for Listeners

1. While the other has the floor, must not interrupt with a reply, opinion, or even nonverbal disagreement with any of speaker's statements.
2. Must reflect back what they understand to be speaker's views (acknowledging and verifying the negative or disagreeable views as well as the positive).
3. Must ask questions to clarify anything they don't understand.
4. When they want to reply, must first check to be sure they have understood correctly and *then* get permission to be the new speaker.

If you haven't already internalized some such set of rules or if you want to polish your use of the techniques of active listening, reading the Appendix would be useful before continuing with this chapter.

How to Coach Active Listening

When you conduct people in active listening, your overt concern may be to facilitate a dialogue about their current issue so as to find a win/win resolution. But there is always at least a secondary goal, if not your most important purpose, of helping them learn to have such dialogues in the future — without your aid, and before they reach a crisis.

Hence every facilitated active listening session is a training session. You are explicitly instructing them in a skill and set of social rules, and you are also providing a role model by your own listening behavior.

At times it becomes appropriate and necessary to put the training agenda first even if it slows down the dialogue. Not only is the training probably more important in the long run than the particular issue at hand, but it's also frankly useful to pull the disputants away from the volatility of their shouting match by transforming it into an orderly, rational communications exercise.

Enlist everyone to help coach one another. Say, for example, when Roger has the floor, "The rest of you, hold up your hand when you hear anyone other than Roger make a statement of opinion or try to take the floor from Roger without repeating his point back to him."

Every time they slip into attributing feelings, opinions, or motives to others, remind them, "*Tell* about yourself; *ask* about the other." If they are familiar with the concept of "I" statements, that phrase reminds them to talk about their own feelings, desires, and difficulties. It helps them avoid "there *you* go again," "*you* always . . . ," "*you* are trying to . . ." and "*you* are . . . [crazy/stupid/cruel/lying]." (There is nothing wrong with the word *you* in sincere questions — "How do you feel about . . . ?" — or in referring to specific events — "When you called me an idiot, I felt hurt.")

A useful training device is to put up an A-I-R chart (Figure 2-3) and point to the three steps each time a listener wants the floor. It also makes a good take-home handout.

Sometimes it helps to say to the speaker, "Pretend you're an investigative reporter trying to find out what Roger really believes and wants. No matter how crazy you may think he is, you're not going to inject your own opinion into the interview. Because this isn't about your position, it's about his position."

Figure 2-3. Clearing the A-I-R.

1. **A**ppreciate

Explicitly tell others that you want to hear their point of view.

"I appreciate this opportunity to discuss the problem with you."
"I may or may not agree with you, but I'm glad to hear your opinion."
"I want to understand you."
"Thank you for coming to me about this."

2. **I**nquire

The other person has the floor. Follow rules for active listening.

"Are you saying that ... "
"Let me be sure I understand your position: ..."
"Can I tell you what I'm hearing so far, and then respond to just that piece before you go on to your second point?"

3. **R**espond

Now you have the floor. You can say anything you want. However, if you want the discussion to be productive, remember:

<u>Tell</u> about yourself; <u>ask</u> about the other.

You might add, "Don't worry, you'll get your opportunity to have the floor."

You'll probably have to stop speakers from giving up the floor too readily.

After listening passively for a few minutes, a listener says, "May I have the floor?"

Gina [*speaker*]: Sure.

Coach: No! Don't give him the floor until you're sure he understood your point.

Gina [*speaker*]: Okay, no [*laughs*], you can't have the floor until you understand what I'm saying.

Tom [*listener*]: I understand what you're saying. Now may I have the floor?

Gina [*speaker*]: Yes, you may.

Coach: No, not yet. You can't know that he understood you just because he says he did. You need him to repeat back what he heard you say.

Tom [*listener*]: You said . . .

Coach: Sorry, let's take it from the top. You, Tom, feel you have heard Gina's point and you'd like to respond, right? Okay, then you need to say, "I heard you saying that . . ." and summarize it back to her. Then ask if you got it right. Then, when you know that she feels she was heard, ask if you can have the floor.

Tom: What if she says no?

Coach: Then you don't really *want* the floor, you see, because if she doesn't feel she was heard, she's certainly not going to be listening to you when it's your turn.

Tom [*listener*]: I heard you saying that I am a male chauvinist because I think the women in this office are here to make the men's lives easier and not vice versa, and also that some of my jokes aren't funny. Right?

Gina [*speaker*]: I didn't just say they aren't funny; I said they are offensive and degrading.

Tom [*listener*]: Offensive and degrading. Now may I have the floor?

Gina: Yes, you may.

Tom [*now speaker*]: Okay, I don't agree that . . .

Coach [*interrupting*]: Well done, both of you! You achieved an exchange of turns. Now, Gina, remember that you are the listener. Tom can now say whatever he decides to say, and you're the investigator trying to learn what his viewpoint might be. I'll help you.

Speakers often try to make more points than listeners can keep track of. Encourage the listeners to attempt asking for the floor as soon as they have heard a chunk of opinion they'd like to respond to and before the speaker goes on to another point.

When interlocutors have trouble remembering who has the floor or keep jumping in with a reaction, I usually use an object like my watch or a throw pillow as a kind of "scepter" for the speaker to hold. "You don't have to wait until you have said everything you want to say before giving up the scepter, but don't give it to Jay until you are sure he has understood the one point so that you'll be able to make yourself listen to his response."

The scepter also works subliminally as a calming device when tempers are out of control. A soft cushion is ideal for that reason. A letter opener, army knife, or baseball bat doesn't work very well.

Validating Both Sides

Readers of this book are probably fairly good at the skill of "joining": reaching out to make another person feel comfortable with you, trust you, and consider you capable of sharing his or her perspective. We make joining moves naturally, subconsciously, many times each day. Joining becomes more challenging, however, in the context of two or more individuals who are in conflict. How do you join with all of them in a balanced, equitable way when they are at odds with each other?

The answer is *not* to avoid taking sides. It is to take sides *alternately* and *selectively*. Everything you say as a mediator will occupy a position sometimes closer to one side, sometimes closer to the other. You need to develop a constant awareness of how and to what purpose you're joining with one, the other, both, or a position beyond either of them.

You are not neutral. Unlike judicial dispute resolution,

Balanced Joining

Unlike a judicial mediator, you are *not* neutral. You *do* take sides; only you join with both sides—alternately and selectively.

---

there is no such thing as a neutral facilitator of harmony within groups. Although you aren't interested in one side winning and one losing, you do have opinions about their respective positions. It is clear to you that antagonist X is "right" about certain points and wrongheaded, or unnecessarily stubborn, about others; whereas Y is "right" to behave in certain ways and just plain silly to be such a stick about some things. If you tried only to facilitate the process, without advocating for the direction you believe to be in their best interest as a group, they wouldn't get the full benefit of your experience and insight— so why should they continue to employ you?

(Incidentally, like active listening, this advice applies not just to Plan A but throughout your dealings with people who aren't dealing well with each other. Join with them *alternately* and *selectively*.)

Figure 2-4 shows a mediator criticizing someone's body language during a dialogue. He approaches antagonist X respectfully and gently, makes the observation as nonjudgmentally as possible, then joins with X momentarily. ("Maybe you didn't realize you were coming across like this.") Immediately, he joins sympathetically with the other antagonist, Y, taking the risk of alienating X. Just when Y is beginning to feel vindicated and self-righteous, however, the mediator turns the tables. He says, in effect, "I felt just as turned off as you did by X's behavior but look how I handled it. Couldn't you do something similar?" Before they know what didn't hit them, the parties hear their mediator joining with the good intentions of X and challenging *both* of them to change.

This technique is an intuitive balancing act; it improves with practice. A beginner is tempted to stay neutral, but you'll lose your status as a trusted facilitator of win/win resolution as surely by failing to acknowledge the right and healthy parts of

Figure 2-4. Balanced joining.

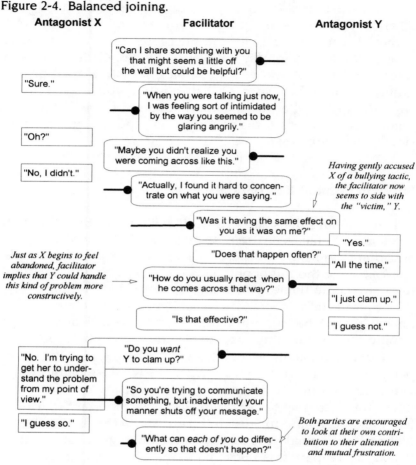

their respective positions as you will if you misjudge how far one party will trust you to support the other.

Remember they really want win/win. Each of them wants you to be sympathetic to the other side as well as their own. They are uncomfortable about the rift between them; they need to reconcile. They are relieved when you model for them the possibility of doing so, helping them reconnect with the parts of themselves that want to respect and cooperate with each other, which their anger has stifled.

You will take sides more provocatively as you cement your alliance with them—as they trust you and rely on your help. Although you'll go further from the center and hang out there longer (sometimes for days or weeks, while people reconsider their positions), always you'll be doing so with a great deal of thought about what aspect of their position you are selectively supporting. It will always be only a matter of time before you rejoin side X or return to the middle ground, hoping to bring side Y back with you.

Win/Win Conflict Resolution

Active listening does not ensure that you will find common goals. It only makes it *possible* to do so. All of the foregoing dos and don'ts are for a purpose in Plan A: to *keep redefining the problem.* If you lose sight of that purpose, you could listen until the cows come home; you could exchange views thoroughly, yet never make progress. The whole group has to keep its eye on the goal (if you are the facilitator, your principal task is to remind them) of finding the *new* idea that works best for all.

Obviously, conflicts don't always end happily for either party. In this age of runaway litigation, win/lose battles often wind up lose/lose, with everyone bloodied except the attorneys. You first have to ask yourself, "Is it important that I defeat the other?" and further, if the answer to that is yes, "Am I willing to risk much loss on my own side to gain that result?" If you are reading this book, you aren't prepared to pay that price. You know that when one side loses, the other side usually turns out also to have lost more than it won. You are looking for the win/win outcome.

Win/win doesn't have to mean compromise—both sides getting less than they had hoped for. The ideal is for the outcome to be even *better* for all than what they might have gained by a win/lose approach. Otherwise, how can we say that "conflict means opportunity"?

Dig deeper, therefore, into what both parties really want. When you discover both full sets of goals, your own and the other's, chances are that they will overlap more than you thought. Redefine the problem and take another look at it. Is it still a conflict? That is, do the parties still seem to want only incompatible outcomes? If so, you can reconsider the "warfare" option (see Figure 1-2), or you can come back once more to dig deeper and reframe the problem and try again. If it no longer appears to be a conflict, then you proceed to attack the problem as a team. You don't need Plans B, C, and so forth, for that particular problem.

Suppose, however, teamwork continues to elude you and the polar opposite—warfare—is still unappealing. You have dug deeper and you have redefined the problem more than once, and you or the people you are trying to help have the distinct feeling that you've exhausted that approach. "We have been here too many times before." Then it isn't just a matter of listening actively and clarifying goals rationally. The group of squabbling individuals, or the whole organization, may need to learn to value differences.

That is the object of Plan B.

3

Plan B: Clarify, Sort, and Value Differences

The problem hasn't gone away. In Plan A, we focused on the parties' common goals, set aside their threats and their unrealistic demands, clarified their most important objectives as specifically as possible, and put those in some kind of rank order. Those steps often *do* reveal win/win solutions (or free people to discover them), but let's assume Plan A didn't accomplish enough. The disputants are still miles apart. Your next approach focuses on the differences that you tried not to be distracted by at first.

Figure 3-1 expands the section of the CRS flowchart (Figure 1-1) that bears the label "Plan B." As was true in Plan A, your goal is still to reframe the problem in such a way that the team can attack it together instead of attacking one another. The strategy of Plan B is to get all the disputants to list every grievance, offense, dispute, and presumed incompatibility they can think of, as shown in Figure 3-1. Take plenty of time. (Of course, the list doesn't really have to be anywhere near complete; conflict resolution is a perpetual, ongoing process.)

The participants don't have to agree that an item belongs on the list. If they disagree about whether something is a problem, it's an important difference of opinion. For example, if some people feel that the engineers and the marketers fail to communicate, put that on the list.

The procedure outlined in Figure 3-1 allows the group to perform a kind of emergency room triage among the various listed complaints: to eliminate the misunderstandings, to increase members' respect and diplomacy toward one another, to

Figure 3-1. Plan B: Clarify, sort, and value differences.

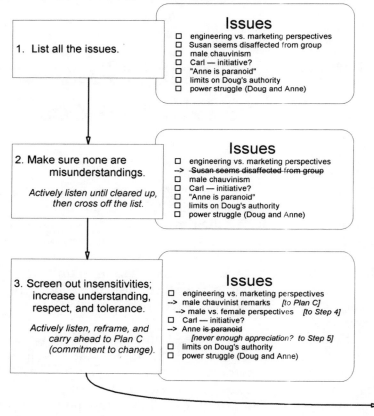

turn diversity into strengths rather than strains, and to call attention to individual problems that cannot be addressed as a group process.

These sorting screens (misunderstanding, insensitivity, point of view, and individual issues) aren't always mutually exclusive. For example, an issue might be partly a matter of misunderstanding, which gets cleared up, and partly of insensitivity, which gets targeted for change, and also could involve diversity in points of view, which should be turned into a strength. Or, a person who consistently offends others may need more than just having his insensitivity pointed out to

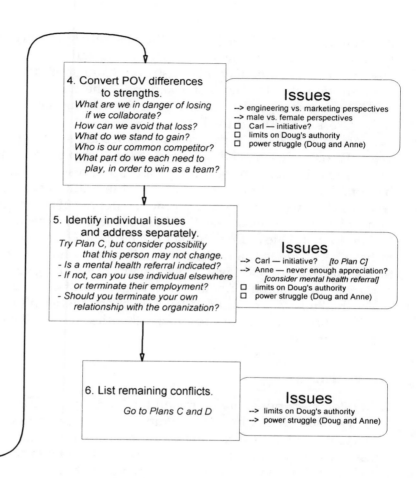

him. His hostile comments might be symptoms of a personality or emotional disorder, problems we shall return to under the heading "Individual Issues."

Let's follow those same hypothetical issues that came up in the goal sorting of Plan A, through the Plan B triage process.

Misunderstandings

Look at the left side of Figure 3-1 (step 2). It turns out that Susan doesn't have intentions of leaving the organization at all.

Far from it! She loves her job; the circumstantial evidence that led to the impression she was unhappy and seriously looking elsewhere was completely misconstrued. "You shouldn't have inferred, you should have just asked me," she says, in the active listening session that follows your list making—and she is right. Cross that one off the list.

You may well doubt that human beings are so straightforward. Perhaps Susan is lying, either to the group or to herself. There must be some reason for people's impression that she had one foot out the door. Nonetheless, the beauty of this procedure is that we don't have to plumb the depths of every question. If Susan chooses to play this hand close to her chest, we'll let her do that. One of three things will happen: (1) It will prove to have been, indeed, a misunderstanding, (2) whatever game Susan was playing, she won't play again, or (3) the issue will surface again in some form, and next time it won't get screened out at the "misunderstanding" level. In short, there isn't much risk in letting a real issue slip by; it will either resolve itself or come around again.

Insensitivities

Other items are not so much misunderstandings as insensitivities. Two such items in our illustration each happen to be an important issue as well as a matter of insensitivity. Male chauvinism is both an unacceptable pattern of debasement, dealt with in step 3 of Figure 3-1, and an opportunity to discuss point of view (POV) differences, which the group will do at length in step 4. Similarly, "Anne is paranoid" is name calling by Carl, but when reframed more sensitively, it is an issue you plan to address with Anne individually (step 5).

You don't need a lesson on treating people with respect, or on the fact that cultural insensitivity is bad for business. I won't rehash what has already been said in several good books about diversity in the workplace and about how stereotyping undermines productivity.[1] Pertinent to our discussion, though, is what happens when you do try to put prejudice aside. What's the first mistake people make when they determine to stretch beyond their prejudices and reach across the sex, race, or cul-

ture gap? They *patronize,* unintentionally and without even being aware that they are doing it. Then, having offended the
other person, their natural next step is to say, "Those people
are paranoid." And there they are again, miles apart.

Mistake: "I'm really glad we have our first female partner, Sandra.
   It's taken this firm longer than most to break the glass ceiling.
   You're lucky there's been so much pressure for it." (*Now why did
   she take offense at that? Women are weird!*)

Mistake: "You don't look Jewish." (*No horns?*)

Mistake: "Say, bro', what's hap'nin'?" (*White guy to black guy—imply-
   ing,* The color of your skin tells me you don't speak standard English.)

These examples show how the *awareness* of another person's gender, nationality, race, or religion (or physical handi-
cap, speech defect, sexual preference, or attractiveness) doesn't
necessarily equate with greater *sensitivity.* (The Monty Python
group used to do a television sketch where a man with an enor-
mous nose came into an office and the official kept saying
things like, "Please sit down, Mr. Nose, er, Smith. . . .")

Is the answer, then, to avoid all references to race, religion,
gender, or disabilities? Not necessarily. In each of the last three
examples—the first woman partner, a Jewish person, and a
white guy talking to a black guy—making no reference at all
would have been preferable. But if you work in an office or
plant where hearing Hispanic music all day drives you crazy,
you should bring it up. The point is to do it in a voice that
implies "we" rather than "you" or "them."

Mistake: "I'm sick of the Latino station you people listen to all
   day."

Better: "I wonder if we could either find a station we all like, or
   develop some sort of rotation system, taking turns as 'radio
   tuner of the day'?"

POV

In filmmaking, POV stands for the camera's point of view. Even
if we were all objective lenses (which we are not), our position

and the direction we are looking would still bias what we see. When others confirm that our observations, analysis, and goals are entirely valid, that only means they share our point of view. The challenge of resolving disagreements often begins with trying to comprehend the problem from the point of view of others who belong to a different group, come to the situation from a different background, or think in a different way.

As I have already suggested, different POVs are a good thing. Differences that look at first like fundamental conflicts can be exactly the opposite, spurs to creativity.

Many kinds of POV differences occur within organizations. All of the following kinds have in common the fact that they potentially enrich the whole team but also tax the limits of mutual understanding.

Style vs. Style

Much is said these days about communication styles, thinking styles, personality "types" (including the popular Myers-Briggs dimensions)—oversimplifications that offer hope to those who struggle to relieve disharmony in organizations. If only there were a system for matching the right types, we could put people who possess certain characteristics together with people who are best at appreciating those characteristics, and who in turn happen to bring the team just those qualities that the others can discern and capitalize upon.

Usually, that doesn't happen. Those whose styles are most different often seek each other out. Invariably, when two people decide to go into business together (or when someone hires a key associate), it's because they possess different talents and skills, complementing one another's. Sooner or later, their differences in communication styles, attitudes, responses to crisis, business philosophies, and long-term goals are bound to frustrate them. If the partnership is to survive, they have to stop being surprised and disappointed about those differences. They must rediscover the value in them. A business partnership requires as much work as any other marriage.

If you are a human resources professional or an organizational consultant, you may already be using personality typing

> Opposites attract—and then can't stand each other.

or "styles" in your work with teams. The following is an effective way to stimulate discussion of any two such personality or communication style dimensions. Show your group the two-axis chart shown in Figure 3-2. Explain that these are only two of the many dimensions along which people differ, but they sometimes lead to interesting insights about difficulties in understanding other people's points of view.

The two-dimensional space plotted on this chart displays only one possible pair of dimensions you might use, depending upon the kinds of POV differences that are relevant in your organization. I find these two dimensions to be most appropriate with cross-functional teams, where communication and thinking styles are often diverse. Placing several different oc-

Figure 3-2. Communication styles exercise: display chart.

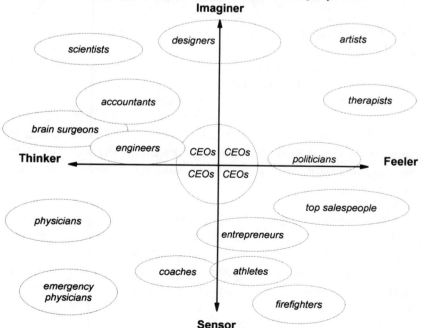

cupational "types" on the chart (without making any scientific claims) helps the group understand what the two dimensions refer to. In Figure 3-2, the Feeler (warm, empathic, emotional) versus the Thinker (cold, rational) horizontal dimension is immediately clear. The vertical dimension needs a little explanation. People whom we call Sensors (as opposed to Imaginers) tend to decide and act quickly, based on immediate reactions to people and events. They are also more domineering and less concerned about others' feelings than the Imaginers, who are the visionaries, speculators, and long-range planners, more idealistic and less concerned with practical details. You might explain to the group, "If your house were on fire, you wouldn't call a scientist or an artist to put it out." You might also say that the best leaders can be found in any quadrant, but probably closer to the center than to any of the extreme types. (This will introduce a little bias into their subsequent judgments, but it's not an objective assessment anyway.)

Then put up a blank chart and ask the whole group in which quadrants they think each individual member belongs (Figure 3-3). Since we all have a range of styles under different circumstances, some individuals may span from one sector to another.

You might ask about others who aren't present, too, such as the CEO of a parent company, the vice president they all report to, or the current boss's predecessor.

Since all four quadrants describe normal, healthy, valuable types of people, I haven't encountered much embarrassment about doing the exercise this way. In fact, you will get fairly quick consensus among all raters, with the possible exception of the person being rated.

The group immediately agrees that Burt is way out on the Feeler end, and more Sensor than Imaginer. "No, I'm not that weird," Burt protests. "I'm more in the middle."

"None of us is just one type," the leader reassures him. "In truth, you probably have a Thinker mode that's dominant at certain times, but the group is telling you they see your Feeler mode more than they see it in other members of this group. The difference

Figure 3-3. Communication styles exercise: finished chart.

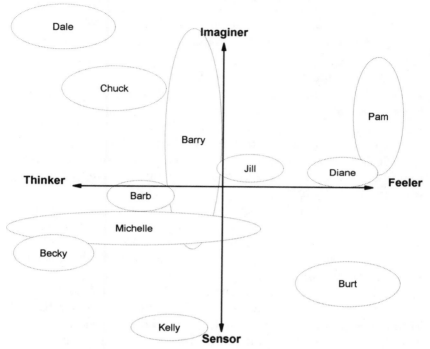

between how you see yourself and how they see you is interesting, isn't it? But let's go on with the exercise."

You don't want to focus on any one individual's style, because this exercise is not about change. Other chapters will deal with change; this is about accepting and benefiting from the different styles that exist.

After placing all the names roughly where they fit on those two dimensions, ask the group whether this display reflects how well people work together. You will find, on the whole, a great deal of correspondence. If Becky is in the lower left quadrant, there you'll see most of the individuals with whom she has the easiest time communicating. In the upper right quadrant will be most of the individuals with whom she feels little connection. But there are exceptions, and you will get to those in a minute. First let people comment on the extent to which the chart has successfully pinpointed the coalitions that exist.

The final step is to explore the exceptions, which will be of two kinds. If a pair of individuals whom you have plotted as very different in styles are good friends or work well together, then ask the question, "What are they doing right?" For they serve as an example of building strength from diversity. They have found a way of giving to their relationship the best that each has to offer, without suffering from their differences in points of view. Discussion will reveal that what they do is acknowledge their different POVs, take delight rather than aggravation from them, and deliberately capitalize on them by learning from one another.

The opposite kind of exception is the pair of individuals in proximity on the chart, who can't stand each other. Has that always been true, or does it date from some event that was poorly handled in the organization? Are they rivals? (See the section Triangling later on in this chapter.) Or are they very dissimilar on some third dimension not shown in this display?

Most business enterprises require fundamentally different kinds of people, not just at the top but all the way down. If you have engineers to design and manufacture products as well as nonengineers who are good at marketing and selling, sooner or later you are going to hear those groups disparaging one another. If you employ creative writers and artists to design advertising campaigns, along with account executives to work with the corporate clients, sooner rather than later you are going to hear the "free spirits" and the "suits" expressing frustration with one another. Airline pilots versus the nonpilots in management; physicians versus hospital administrators—frequently it is the people with the technical expertise versus those who know how to organize a business, bring products to market, or maintain cash flow. In all such cases, what they say about each other is the same thing men and women say about the opposite sex: "They just don't get it."

The communication styles exercise merely serves as a launching point for discussion of how to make those POV differences a team asset. We'll continue that discussion as we consider some other kinds of POV differences as well.

Male vs. Female

Where communications are concerned, the term *point of view* doesn't begin to do justice to the differences between men and women. In many ways the gender POV differences cut across cultures, languages, and age groups. Yet the male/female partnership works in the closest and most successful kind of human organization, the family; and even in business organizations, we can point to more examples of successful collaboration between men and women than unsuccessful. What better proof of the proposition that fundamental differences can be strengths?

Issues of sexist bias and of sexual harassment between men and women fall under the headings of insensitivities and individual issues. (A pattern of sexist behavior isn't a "point of view," it's a symptom of neurosis or a personality disorder.) In this section, though, we are talking about differences in how men and women tend to *view* situations. Furthermore, we're interested in differences both real and imagined. What men believe to be true about women, and what women believe to be true of men, is just as big a factor in undermining teamwork as anything that might be true in some more objective sense.

Individual differences among people of the same sex are greater than any difference between the masculine persuasion and the feminine. Furthermore, it isn't at all clear that the sex differences we generalize about are the most important ones or that they won't change over time or in another society. What matters for purposes of this book is what you do about such differences if they are felt to exist in your organization. For example, if both women and men tend to believe men are less understanding about relationships than women are, a consequence of that belief could be that they might overvalue a woman's assessment of a particular interpersonal situation; or if she disagrees with someone's proposed course of action, her judgment might be discounted as too sensitive.

There is probably some truth to that generalization about women's sensitivity to the fabric of relationships, and about men's preferring to believe that connections are simpler and more ordered. There is truth, also, in the proposition that men are less willing or able to tolerate situations that leave them exposed and vulnerable—to attack, to criticism, to humiliation, to rejection.

On the other hand, no research supports the common generalization that men are out of touch with their own feelings and insensitive to how others feel. Although significant numbers of men may feel uncomfortable when vulnerable to emotions like hurt, fear, despair, and rage, the truth is that men are just as perceptive about the *unspoken* feelings expressed between the lines by other men as women are about other women's feelings. The problem is that both sexes seem to need more explicit statements of what is on the mind and in the heart of a person of the opposite sex, whereas they are better at intuiting the feelings of a member of their own sex. Thus both sexes find themselves frequently mystified and misunderstood by the opposite sex.

When male/female differences manifest themselves in work relationships, *what can you do about them?* As with other POV differences, refer to these questions:

- ❏ What do we really fear losing if we collaborate?
- ❏ How can we collaborate *without* losing those valuable differences?
- ❏ What do we stand to gain by working together?
- ❏ Who is our common competitor?
- ❏ What do we each need to do in order to get the benefits of teamwork?

Culture vs. Culture

A large international advertising agency purchased a small but highly successful and well-reputed agency in the Northwest. The latter's eighty employees had printed slogans in their offices like ALL WORK AND NO SKIING MAKES JACK A DULL BOY and CREATIVITY IS 10 PERCENT INSPIRATION AND 90 PERCENT PERSPIRATION—SO LET'S GO BACKPACKING. This was not the way the chairman in New York viewed the business. He loved to quote the policy that was widely attributed to a major competitor, Jay

Chiat: "If you aren't coming in on Saturday, don't bother to show up for work on Sunday." His idea of sensitivity to employees' personal and family needs was to pay them handsomely and provide generous health benefits; but woe betide the writer or executive who left a meeting at seven in the evening for his child's basketball game.

Not that the chairman would know when that happened four levels down in the organization. That is the great thing about organizational culture: The leaders convey their expectations in a variety of ways (some less subtle than others), and members create norms of behavior to conform with those expectations.

Was this particular culture clash the kind of POV difference that could be turned into a strength? Probably not. It sounds like an incompatibility that will require Plan C. If, on the other hand, the acquired agency were Spanish-speaking and located in Mexico City, it wouldn't be a matter of which culture should prevail but of how to share the benefits of both, for each client and project.

> *"Strength From Diversity" Questions*
> 1. What are we in danger of losing if we collaborate?
> 2. How can we avoid that loss?
> 3. What do we stand to gain?
> 4. Who is our common competitor?
> 5. What parts do we each need to play, in order to win as a team?

The five "strength from diversity" questions will help you deal with culture clash as with personality styles, even though the differences in culture have little or nothing to do with personality. They have to do with the histories of the two organizations, but you aren't going to rewrite history and you don't need to wrestle with its effects. What you want to do is put that diversity to work. When the merger works, the resulting blend should be greater than the sum of the ingredients. That, after all, is why one company acquires or merges with another in the first place.[2]

Too Old vs. Too Young

In any organization, some members have dwelled on earth longer than others. POV differences arise with the need to balance the prudence and experience of elders with the energy, iconoclasm, and questioning of youth.

In a ten-year-old company or a young department, the "rising stars" may be under age 30; in a business whose founder is in his seventies, it's the fifty-year-olds who are champing at the bit. In either case, though, resolving the problem is a matter of getting the best from both generations. When they ask themselves the "strength from diversity" questions, they will find that their fears are specific to their stages of life. "Am I (thought to be) over the hill?" the CEO asks himself. "Then if I give this young man more authority, will he try to shove me out altogether? Will he bankrupt the company, wiping out the value of my stock? I had better resist that!"

The would-be successor wonders, "Will I have to wait decades to be recognized as a leader? If every move I make is seen as a threat, how can I ever prove my own competence? On the other hand, if he thinks I'm weak, he'll never respect me. I had better fight with him!"

This is a classic case of what I call counter-leaning, a frequent result of POV differences. We'll discuss it shortly.

Be aware, also, that some people carry family baggage irrationally into nonfamily relations, sometimes with surprising hostility and contempt. Rage or disappointment with their own parents or children distorts their communication with others of that generation. (See The Seven Deadly Isms in the section Individual Issues.)

Language, Race, and Religion

Between-*group* distrust or hostility shapes between-*person* interactions in the workplace more than anywhere else—if we let it. It is also true that unhappy interactions with individual persons can lead to negative attitudes about groups, which then perpetuate themselves. The resulting tension drains productivity until people have the courage to transcend those barriers.

We have already discussed, under Insensitivities, examples of how hard it is to resist the easy recourse to prejudice in the workplace. But suppose you don't have that problem. Your organization includes people of different backgrounds who do, by and large, respect each other. However, that does not mean they understand each other's points of view or derive any benefits from their diversity. They may tend to avoid antagonism by denying their differences. This is actually dangerous, because it stops you from anticipating conflicts before they get out of hand. And you lose the opportunity to capitalize on the different points of view or experiences. Therefore it is worth opening up these questions even if they aren't on anyone's list of interpersonal problems or issues.

"I notice no one has put anything on the list that has to do with our different ethnic backgrounds. Yet it's clear to all of us that we've got a whole rainbow here. Do we ever get into any situations where we look at problems differently because we're coming from different backgrounds? Is that a liability or an asset to the group?"

*   *   *   *   *

In summary, whether differences in POV are due to background, personal styles, gender, organizational cultures, or internal competition for resources, your first step is to learn how things look from the other group's or person's POV. (If you are a mediator, your first step is to facilitate that learning.) Active listening not only achieves a certain amount of understanding but also *displays* each party's understanding to the others. Then the different factions decide whether they have more to gain by teamwork than to lose by collaborating with "those guys."

Strength in Diversity

Now let's look at three techniques, beyond active listening, for finding strength in diversity. The two most important techniques for turning what appear to be incompatible differences into positives are the reframe, which I introduced in Chapter 2, and what I call the un-leaning operation. Reframing has many variations, of which I shall discuss two: the positive reframe and triangling.

Positive Reframe

Compare these negative and positive ways of referring to essentially the same facts:

Mistake: "Gary is so uptight about taking risks that he shoots me down before I've even fleshed out my ideas."
Better: "Gary helps keep my feet on the ground when I get carried away with some of my big ideas."

Mistake: "Sarah has her blue-sky vision of the way she wants to believe things are, but you can't rely on her to focus on the details."
Better: "Sarah is the one we rely on for the big picture; I tend to get lost sometimes in the details."

Mistake: "Charlie is a mental plodder. If he can't see it on a spread-sheet, he doesn't get it."
Better: "Charlie is great at thinking things through analytically."

Mistake: "Michelle thinks everything's a joke."
Better: "We'd be lost without Michelle's sense of humor."

Mistake: "Bill's getting on in years, and he doesn't realize the world has changed."
Better: "Bill's seen a lot of fads come and go in this industry, and he brings the more long-term perspective to our meetings."

Each of these examples is a positive reframe. Reframing is the kind of medicine spin doctors practice in political campaigns. It's a basic therapeutic technique, a basic sales technique, and also a natural way most people have of talking to others when they want to be nice. You don't have to be a psychologist to see that it's a good technique to use when people are arguing with each other. You've already used it, in active listening, in the Appreciate step of "clearing the A-I-R" (Figure

2-3). But it's also indispensable for getting people to see that their differences are possible strengths instead of incompatibilities.

The easiest place to use reframes is when you're facilitating debate between two or more people. You hear them being critical, defensive, or pessimistic, and you're creative enough to suggest a more optimistic interpretation of their difference. It's a little harder when you are a target of someone's diatribes. It may be hardest of all to develop the habit of reframing your own mental attitude, not just the diplomatic words but the actual thoughts. But the skill of positive reframing does become natural with practice.

Triangling

A disproportionate number of conflicts arise in situations where there are three principals. A and B agree that C is the real source of their problems. Then A and C reconcile, agreeing with one another that the real troublemaker is B, until B makes her peace with C. But then A is the alien. As each corner of a triangle is directly opposite the side that joins the other two corners, each member of a triangle provides a potential opponent to the relationship between the other two.

Sibling rivalry is an example of this kind of conflict. But jealousy and competition for attention, resources, or approval are certainly not restricted to brothers and sisters. "Sibling rivalry" goes on in all organizations, when people who aren't actually related to one another take on the roles of jealous or competitive siblings within the organizational "family." (It's even more intense if they *are* related.)

Although group members make their lives more difficult when they triangle each other, a change agent can actually exploit this powerful human tendency to shift people quickly from opponents to allies by reminding them of their common problems with a third party.

For example, in mediating "sibling" disputes, one can usually bring the parties together almost immediately by triangling the parent or boss as their common problem. That has to be done carefully, though, to be effective.

In working with Ed and Susan, a squabbling foundation director and associate director, the consultant suggested that part of
the problem might be the way the board and its president com-
municated with both of them. At first, Ed and Susan took charac-
teristically opposite positions on that question. However, when
the consultant asked whether the board members had a clear perception of which executive they should call with what concerns,
both executives said no and blamed the president for that. "Clarity
and specificity are not Joe's strong points," Ed said, and Susan
said that was an understatement. Then she made reference to
some event they both remembered with laughter, and the change
in tone was astonishing. Had someone made a film clip of the next
few minutes of the session, no viewer would have guessed that
these were the same two people who were convinced they could
never work together.

The consultant pointed out that here was something they
agreed on. How could they get Joe to clarify their roles to the
board? They both said they didn't think there was any chance of
Joe changing. "I've learned," the consultant advised, "never to say
no for someone else. But if your prediction turns out to be accu-
rate, what can you do (instead of continuing to blame each other
for the problem) to make sure you maintain the clarity and specificity on your end?"

One must administer just the right dose of this medicine,
because an overdose can cause harmful side effects, possibly
fatal to the team. Get them on the same side, but don't leave
them agreeing to hate the common enemy. That would only
result in their slipping back to fight with each other again,
prompted by shared fears of where their anger at the authority
figure might lead (see Chapter 5). Instead, once common
ground has been established, move the discussion on to the
question, "What do we need to do in order to improve things
with X [the "parent" or boss]?" That will lead to later steps
(Plans C and D), which might directly involve the third party
and others.

Whether you are a protagonist or a mediator, the key is to
shift relatively soon to *what people can do together, constructively,
to solve the problem they both have with another person.* Even if there

is no way that person is going to change (for example, she is their mother and she has been doing this to them for forty years), that still doesn't mean they have to allow her behavior to split them.

> Simply agreeing that the "parent" is the problem isn't telling them anything they don't know. You have to go beyond that to the insight that their perceived differences are largely a defense or a way of coping with that situation and that they *can* deal with it more effectively.

You can also use the "common enemy" technique when you yourself are one of the protagonists in a dispute:

Mistake: "What are you going off on me for? It's Paula who tells you one thing and tells me another. Yell at her!"

Better: "Could you and I prevent this from happening in the future if we give each other the benefit of the doubt and check it out with each other every time we get some weird message from Paula?"

Un-Leaning

Un-leaning is my name for an antidote to counter-leaning, which does not mean leaning on counters. Counter-leaning refers to the fact that human beings have a tendency to overcompensate for one another by leaning too far in opposite directions.

The most familiar example of the phenomenon of counter-leaning is between parents. Jack is too authoritarian with the children; Jill tries to compensate by being more lenient than she would otherwise be; Jack reacts by being even more rigid and punitive; she leans even more toward softness and inconsistency. The children go nuts. Exactly the same thing can happen between business partners. Hank believes they have to give their employees every tool they need to be productive; his partner, Russ, believes if they want to be profitable they'd better not upgrade their computers until absolutely necessary; Hank interprets that to mean Russ is going to stand in the way of every purchase, so he'd better not consult Russ; Russ figures that means he'd better resist every purchase Hank wants to make, in hopes of blocking at least 25 percent of them; so Hank jacks up his proposed outlays by 40 percent. The whole company goes nuts.

In other words, valid differences of opinion can amplify themselves to ridiculous extremes. The initial perceptions aren't necessarily distortions, but as each party tries to compensate for the other, they react to exaggerated fears of how dangerously the other might act. With amazing rapidity, those fears become self-fulfilling prophecies. The image that comes to mind is of a tiny boat being tipped one way and the other by two people who are trying to balance one another's off-center weight. As each perceives the other overcompensating, the amplitude of the boat's wobbling only increases. Soon they are no longer in the same boat—they are swimming.

> If you are leaning over to starboard to balance the boat against the other guy's propensity to lean too far to port, both of you are about to get wet.

This phenomenon, counter-leaning, produces misunderstandings, exaggerates POV differences, and frequently creates the appearance of intractable individual issues. The cure is unleaning. Your job is to get the parties to take the small risk of refraining from leaning quite so far to counterbalance one another. This process has to be conscious, watching for occasions when either party anticipates the other's excessiveness. If they are sailing a small boat together, one of them agrees to sit where he is, leaving it to the other to balance the boat.

Hank and Russ realize that they've been overcompensating for their worst fears about one another's irrationality. [I am "Ken," as this happens to be an actual meeting with a pair of my clients.]

Hank: If you dismiss my demands because you think they're a ploy, you'll make some bad mistakes. In the interest of curtailing that chain reaction, how about if I pledge myself to only call for new equipment when I'm sincerely convinced it's necessary? You can continue to question me or whomever, until you see that I'm not padding the list of necessities any longer (as I admit I did in the past).

Russ: I *should* stop assuming that anything you do is a ploy. But don't expect me to change overnight, please. I need to get there slowly. So if I call you back and ask you to walk me through your reasoning, or if I ask some questions of the employee concerned, you need to give me the benefit of the doubt and assume I'm not doing it just to resist you.

Ken: Actually, he doesn't have to assume anything. He can just ask you.

Hank: I can tell you right now that if I say we've got to have it—a computer, for example—that means I've already taken the time to question the employee and made a very conservative decision.

Russ: Okay, but shouldn't I perform my function of conservatively questioning all purchases?

Hank: Just don't go overboard.

Ken: You could both spell out what steps Russ will take when following through on a purchase decision by Hank. And every time such an occasion arises, you could spell out precisely *by when* Russ will either have found a more economical way of achieving the same benefits more cheaply or will have made the purchase.

Russ: Actually, I don't think we would have any disagreements if Hank would just give me the benefit of the thinking process he's already gone through, instead of leaving me a one-sentence message.

Hank: Done. Let's shake on it.

What Hank and Russ have done here, with slight nudges from their consultant, is to agree not to lean reflexively in opposite directions. Taking Russ out of the loop altogether would have been a terrible solution because his "waste not, want not" philosophy is vital to the company's survival. The two men will continue to benefit from their different personality styles while they have reclaimed control over their synergy. (Note: All they have achieved here is an oral agreement, of which they can re-mind one another as they struggle to change their actual behav-ior.)

Again, whether you're one of the counter-leaners or a third party who is trying to get them to start un-leaning, you will find occasions to make skilled use of the positive reframe. Russ did so in his last comment, reframing Hank's solo deci-sion-making style as "the benefit of the thinking process he's already gone through."

Individual Issues

We now arrive at step 5 of Figure 3-1. The last group of differ-ences we can remove from the table are those that stem from individuals' psychological status. Some of those may be mental health problems, which sometimes warrant referring the indi-vidual to an appropriate professional—or seeking help your-self, if you are that individual. Others are normal, unavoidable issues that happen to affect one member of the organization more than others. The group isn't necessarily the best context in which to address these issues; yet they need to be talked about at least enough so they don't continue to be sources of fruitless interpersonal conflict.

Types of Individual Issues

Several distinct kinds of individual problems can create or inflame interpersonal conflicts in organizations. Let me de-scribe some of them and then discuss the delicate art of distin-guishing individual issues from those differences that must be worked on as a group.

Certain fundamental *mental health problems* make people ir-ritable, defensive, and/or argumentative. Someone who seems "difficult" may actually be suffering from a mood disorder (anxiety, depression, or manic-depressive illness) or an addic-tive disorder (alcoholism, drug abuse, compulsive gambling, etc.). If you suspect that any of those may be a factor in an individual's conflictive behavior, get a professional evaluation; team problem solving would probably not be effective.

Entitlement is a more lifelong individual issue that leads to interpersonal conflict. The word means appearing to believe that one has either already earned, or shouldn't have to earn, some limited resource such as money, authority, status, or love. Paradoxically, those who protest the loudest that they aren't getting what they are entitled to are often insecure about what they deserve.

Alec, a district manager, is passed over for promotion to the regional manager's job. Stung, he refuses to take the disappointment gracefully. He faxes an angry memo to his boss's superior and spouts conspiracy theories to everyone who will listen.

Zeke is in exactly the same position, and he also refuses to take the disappointment lying down, but his response is simply to write a dignified letter of resignation, without burning any bridges.

Which man has the entitlement issue? Alec. Which man really believes he deserved the promotion? Zeke, of course. Learning that the organization won't offer the advancement he seeks, Zeke looks elsewhere, without too much damage to his inner confidence. Alec desperately needed the promotion to compensate for his lacking inner sense of worth and capability. Now he even more desperately needs to assert his entitlement. Sad to say, that same false sense of entitlement may have cost him the promotion in the first place, as it led him to take his job for granted and reject responsibility. Beneath a false sense of entitlement and excessive concerns about guarding one's prerogatives usually lurks a grave insecurity about self-worth.

When one party in a dispute uses words like *deserve* and *fair* to make his case while no one else involved sees any unfairness, there may be an individual issue of entitlement. In a family business situation, where a member acts as though the privileges of ownership should come to him as his birthright, without having to be earned "the hard way," that entitlement problem most likely originated among the very family members he is in conflict with. Their family business needs family therapy. But that isn't Alec's situation. His entitlement issue goes back to his own family of origin. His current employer has neither the responsibility nor the ability to solve those problems today.

Paranoia is like a tumor that takes root in the mind and, growing, poisons the individual's whole psychology. Paranoid personality disorder is only one of a number of character disorders, but I make special mention of it because conflict with others is an inevitable byproduct and, unfortunately, a perpetuator of paranoia. Acute paranoid behavior and other forms of psychosis can be temporary (and curable) symptoms of many neurophysiological conditions. But the *paranoid personality* is chronic, and there isn't, as yet, any reliable cure. The problem is that paranoids regard as their worst enemies anyone who tells them they're suffering from paranoia and need help.

Someday, a genius will discover a therapy that works on people who refuse to believe they have anything wrong with them (including, along with the character disorders, all those suffering from denial of alcoholism and other addictions). In the meantime, all you can do is help everyone else in the organization to stop maintaining and exacerbating the problem. The message to them must be, "Harry isn't going to change his tune. Can you ignore it and make changes yourselves so that he isn't able to make life hell for you? If not, you need to give him an ultimatum and you need to be prepared to follow through with it and terminate his membership in the group."

Envy is a less severe problem than paranoia, because many cases of envy and rivalry are very responsive to insight. Like the other six deadly sins—gluttony, lust, avarice, and so on— envy is a *natural* toxin, present in all of us. If it seems to be a particularly big problem for someone in the group you are working with, bring it up explicitly. At best, doing so may lead to an individual's awareness that others see his or her envy, prompting an interest in psychotherapy to get over such feelings. At worst, the discussion won't hurt, and it may move the issue off your list of real conflicts.

Fear of change is also a problem we all share to some extent. Everyone advocates change—in everyone else. Some of us like to think of ourselves as flexible folks who are good at changing, but we're probably kidding ourselves. It is very, very hard to change even the things we dislike about ourselves and are embarrassed about, let alone the things that don't cause us any distress. Not only is it hard, it is terrifying, because one never knows what those changes might leave us vulnerable to. After all, the very people we are defending ourselves against are asking us to put aside our defenses.

Nonetheless, many individuals are capable of acknowledging their fear of change, discussing it, and addressing it fairly rationally. If you have gone so far as to identify fear of change as an issue, you may have just taken the biggest and hardest step toward resolving it. The person or persons who are willing to acknowledge their fear of change have nothing to lose but the fear itself, and much to gain from the greater support of other group members.

"The truth is," Bill, a business owner, admitted to his designated successors at a strategic planning retreat, "I just hate like hell to give up the way I've been doing things all these years. It's like a security blanket. When you talk to me about a state of the art plant from the ground up, financed against future earnings, I just see the Awesome Unknown."

"Well, maybe that's a good enough reason not to do it," one of the next-generation managers said. "If Bill isn't comfortable with it, . . ."

"No, it's *not* a good enough reason," Bill said. "It's a reason for me to raise every objection I can think of, but if you guys have thought it through and have an answer to all my objections, we'll do it. I just want you to know it isn't going to be easy."

The Seven Deadly Isms

A set of easily identified individual issues are *the seven deadly isms* that sour relationships within organizations. They are sexism, racism, ageism, chauvinism, elitism, favoritism, and (the worst, in my book) individualism. All may be shared, of course, by many members and are often part of the institutional culture, but any of these deadly isms can just as easily lurk within the poisoned mind of a single individual. What they all have in common is that they incline us to think of others as "those guys" rather than allies.

I'll single out favoritism and individualism for special treatment, but let's look at the first five isms as a group. They involve the conscious or unconscious belief that you can judge an individual's fitness for performance on the basis of gender, race, age, national origin (chauvinism), or privileged background (elitism). (What follows applies also to discrimination against homosexuals and against people with disabilities that are irrelevant to the jobs for which they are applying.)

It is important to distinguish between an *ism* and a mere *generalization* about group differences. Generalizations that have statistical validity are not isms. An ism assumes that the generalization applies to an individual. That assumption is only sometimes illegal but is always illogical. For example, it is true that men consistently score significantly higher than women on tests of spatial visualization ("How would the sides of this box look if they were unfolded to make a two-dimensional figure?"). It is not sexist to report that fact, nor would it be sexist to require a high score on such a test as a condition for employment in a box design factory, even though the test discriminates. What is sexist is to skip the test of spatial ability and use a gender test instead: "No women need apply, because women are inferior in spatial abilities." That would exclude from candidacy the many women whose skills surpass the average man, notwithstanding the chromosomal trend.

Isms affect personal conflict within organizations in more complex ways than just discrimination in hiring. The manifestations may take the form of doubts about people's loyalty or credibility; very subtle stereotyping; or acts of omission, such as not bothering to include someone in a brainstorming session. If such bias recurs after repeated discussion, someone with the authority to do so may have to raise the question of whether the prejudiced individual should continue as a member of the team.

Favoritism is probably inevitable in any organization. It isn't a problem unless it reaches such a degree that people consistently complain about it. If only one person charges the orga-

nization with favoritism, it may actually be an entitlement problem in the complainer.

If you are the one who is regarded as playing favorites,
consider the likelihood that it may be true—and unproductive
for your organization. Do you have *performance* reasons for giving certain individuals the plum assignments? If so, let others
know your basis for those decisions, so as to motivate them to
compete for the opportunities. On the other hand, if you have
been playing favorites for any other reason, then you haven't
been doing a good job of developing your whole team. You
should be grateful for that feedback.

Individualism is one of the mixed blessings of American society. I list individualism among the seven deadly isms because
the philosophy of "taking care of number one" or "meeting my
needs" or just plain selfishness is simply the opposite of teamwork. Don't fall into the trap of believing that enlightened self-
interest is the key to capitalist success. Truly enlightened self-
interest sees that "I need to do whatever I can to help my teammates do their jobs better." (The need to keep individualism in
balance is discussed in depth in Chapter 7.) An individual who
argues otherwise is defending against intrapsychic issues that
are not of the group's making and not for the group's resolving.

> When the story of our age is written, will it be called The
> Triumph of Teamwork Over Individualism? Or The Failure
> of Teamwork in a Culture of Narcissism?

Handling Individual Issues

In this section, I'll assume that you are either an outside
facilitator or an authority figure (not a peer), having diagnosed
an individual issue in a member of the organization. If you ignore that issue, you'll at best fail to do your job. But the risk
may be much greater than that, especially if the behavior you
see is really a symptom of psychopathology (a disordered mind
or a very fragile ego).

This does not mean that you have to be a clinical psychologist or a psychiatrist to tread in the area of individual issues. Plan B creates a framework for delicacy in dealing with them. You won't stir up more than is appropriate to deal with in the organization. However, you must be prepared to move people out of the organization rather than tiptoe around their psychopathologies.

The first step in doing that is to try insights along the lines of the foregoing pages. The better the parties' mental health, the better the chance that they will make constructive use of some insight about the ways their own agendas have been making things difficult for others. If that doesn't happen, though, you have to make some choices, acting gently but firmly:

❏ For mental health issues, an appropriate person can make a professional referral. The most effective way is to require professional help as a condition of further employment. That may be effective as an implied threat, stating your recommendation positively rather than explicitly. (Offer hope: "Others with the same problem have been helped.") If your tact meets with evasion, then be more explicit. Set a time limit for both the onset of treatment and the evaluation of its effects.

❏ Of course, it only makes sense to recommend therapy if the individual's value to the organization outweighs the cost of waiting and the uncertainty of seeing positive changes. If not, and if you are in a position of authority and have already given fair warning, obviously you can simply weed the individual out of your organization or transplant him to another group, as you would a rosebush that doesn't add beauty to its setting.

❏ Short of that, if you're sure that the chances of getting the individual to change are nil but that it won't be possible to terminate his or her employment in the near future, you might skip to Chapter 6 (Plan E) and see what you can do unilaterally to alleviate problems.

❏ On the other hand, if you aren't ready to give up, try the exercises in Chapter 4 as a test of the individual's capacity to change (Plan C). That still leaves open the three options (mental health referral, termination, or your own departure) pending the results of the test.

❑ Finally, another case for Plan C is one in which you feel certain the individual *won't* change, but it is important to let other group members see there is no hope. They will then either conclude, as a group, to terminate the individual or to go ahead to Plan E and try changing unilaterally.

If all that sounds coldly systematic, it is. Nowhere is it more important to be thoughtful, cautious, and deliberate than in isolating an individual rotten apple from the barrel. The consequences of a mistake either way are severe. Falsely to identify an individual as the cause of problems that are really organizational is not only unjust, it is sure to be destructive, as you lose his or her positive contributions and strengthen the group's tendency to scapegoat its *next* identified villain. On the other hand, you must not fail to deal with any individual whose misdirected personal issues are truly destructive to the organization. Hence the need for a flowchart approach (Figure 3-1), or the above checklist, and careful consultation with appropriate professional advisors including a psychologist or psychiatrist, your employee assistance or personnel director, and—not infrequently—the company's attorney.

Remaining Conflicts

Chances are, after screening out all the foregoing kinds of differences for special treatment, one or more serious issues still remain on the list your organization members made at the beginning of this chapter. An example would be a "sibling rivalry" problem, such as the power struggle between Doug and Anne (Figure 3-1). This is not a matter of misunderstanding or insensitivity or point of view. Let us assume that the triangling technique helped clarify how central their boss is to any solution, but it didn't solve the problem. The rivalry could have any of a number of underlying causes, which we may need to explore (Plan D). But first we'll go to Plan C and see if either of the rivals is interested in changing.

Notes

1. R. Roosevelt Thomas, Jr., *Beyond Race and Gender: Unleashing the Power of Your Total Workforce by Managing Diversity* (New York: AMACOM, 1991); Lee Gardenswartz and Anita Rowe, *Managing Diversity.* (Homewood, Ill.: BusinessOne Irwin, 1992).
2. A book that does justice to the many human resources complications of mergers and acquisitions is Anthony Buono and James Bowditch, *The Human Side of Mergers and Acquisitions* (San Francisco: Jossey-Bass, 1989).

4

Plan C: Gain Commitment to Change

Plan B enabled you to eliminate a number of extraneous misunderstandings and reframe some differences as strengths. However, it is likely that a number of those issues you clarified and sorted will require changes that don't come easily. Merely identifying a matter of insensitivity doesn't necessarily throw a "sensitive" switch inside the offender. Point of view differences can't always be reframed as strengths without individuals changing their attitudes and modes of communication.

One team member is obsessive about detecting and correcting flaws while his equally intense colleague, impatient to get product out the door, insists, "Nothing is perfect." Reframing their complementary personality styles as a strength of the team is well and good; but one of them (if not both) still has to be willing to change.

Another way Plan B may lead directly to Plan C is that the boss may have targeted an individual behavior or personality problem as a matter of "fix or fire." Chapter 3 clarified it; now we have to change it.

Finally, fundamental conflicts of interest may still remain ("Meeting my goals is incompatible with meeting your goals") after all is said and done in Plan B.

Chances are, the members of your group are still blaming others and demanding changes in the others' behavior. The smoother members acknowledge that they themselves aren't perfect and, yes, they'll consider doing what they can to re-solve the problem, but only after so-and-so changes first.

Plan C is designed to establish, pragmatically, whether parties to a conflict have any chance of breaking away from mutual antagonism and finger pointing to approach their problems as a team. The principle is both simple and profound: *People who can't admit they are part of the problem will never be part of its solution.* It's hard enough to change our own behavior a little, even when we acknowledge our contribution to the problem and we're really committed to change. Without that commitment, forget it.

Individual Change and Organizational Change

Are we talking about change in individual persons or in that amorphous system of overlapping relationships we call the "organization"? What *is* organizational change, anyway? Is it even meaningful to talk about the behavior of an organization? The truth is, the entities that do the behaving, and therefore the only real objects that can change, are the individual members of the organization. If we want the "organization" to start functioning as a team, that means we want individual people to stop fighting with each other and to behave more cooperatively.

On the other hand, groups exert rapid and powerful effects on how individuals behave. Any one individual has only a modest, slow impact in leading the group as a whole to change.

The best strategy, therefore, is to settle for small steps in whatever appears to be a constructive direction, by whoever appears willing to try those small steps. The group isn't going to change en masse. Waiting for anyone else, much less waiting for *everyone* else to change, is never a good idea. There is no alternative but to take those small steps.

Think of a sports team. Suppose you come in as the new coach. You find that the team hasn't been performing as well as it could because the competitive spirit between and among team members is excessive. All athletes are competitive by nature, of course, but the norms on this team include putting each other down, refraining from complimenting each other publicly or privately, and going for individual records at the expense of winning strategies (shooting instead of passing, for example, if it's basketball). So you tell the team to change, and the team changes, right?

Wrong. You can tell the whole team to change, and every member might agree with you, but all those habits of interaction and all their mutual expectations are too powerful. Most of the individuals, most of the time, continue to behave with one another as they are used to doing. So you call their attention to that individual behavior each time you see it. You use whatever sanctions you have at your command, and you use all your powers of persuasion until gradually one or two of the members behave differently once or twice. Some of the others see that, and they move a little in the direction of more teamwork, which encourages their teammates. Eventually the process accelerates, new norms do get established, and the team, as a team, has changed. But it happened in individual players and not all at once.

Individual change against the norms of a group is very hard to produce, especially if the social context is the same. (In the example I just gave, the players would be even more resistant if it weren't a new coach leading them.) However, once the ball is rolling and the organizational norms are moving in a new direction, then all the pressure is on the individuals to conform with those changes. We say they're "climbing on the bandwagon," "getting with the program," "getting religion," "not rocking the boat," and so forth.

In other words, organizational dynamics are resistant to change early in the process of conflict resolution but eventually become its moving forces.

Agents for change can and must use those facts about human nature. Initially, to overcome the system's powerful inertia, don't fight the most resistant members. Join with those who are interested in change but who haven't felt it was possible. Reframe their problem, sell them adaptive solutions by whatever argument you can employ, and support their small steps in the right direction. Build on those steps until there is enough support for them in the group itself so that peer pressure mounts in favor of change and the more recalcitrant members come along.

At your first opportunity, rent the classic film *Twelve Angry Men* and view it in connection with this book. Henry Fonda plays a juror who is a little less susceptible to peer pressure than the other eleven and who happens to have been unconvinced by the prosecution's arguments to convict a young man of murder. At first Fonda is the outlyer, subject to scorn, but as one juror after another switches his vote, the group pressure shifts overwhelmingly against the *last* man left holding what had originally been a nearly unanimous opinion. Both the script and the twelve actors' performances capture many fundamental processes of human interaction.

If you took a college psychology course, you probably read about the experiments by Asch and others, in which subjects had to answer objective perceptual questions such as which line in a set of three was the same length as a target line or which of two shapes had the larger area. Unknown to the subjects, all the others who answered before them were confederates of the experimenter, instructed to make unanimous choices that were patently wrong. Typically, in such studies, the hapless victim of group pressure goes along with the wrong answer as much as a third of the time, without protesting overtly (but with much internal distress). Furthermore, in some studies researchers were even able to manipulate subjects into denying they had altered their judgments; they *believed* the answers they had given under social pressure. The conformity was much higher when the questions were about matters of opinion rather than measurable fact, but Asch's work showed how the pressure to "go along" can often outweigh even the evidence of our senses.

In real life, in the group whose conflicts you need to resolve, the first person to change his or her position will be like the unfortunate subject in one of those experiments. The second person, though, is in nowhere near so precarious a position. It is much, much easier to resist the majority when you are not the only one doing so. As that slightly uncomfortable minority swells and becomes the majority, change becomes easier for the individuals who resisted it at first. Plan C is based on that insight about human behavior in groups.

All of us are more comfortable behaving as we have behaved in the past and in conformity with our group's norms. The hardest individual changes are the unilateral ones—the ones made by leaders. The leaders must overcome both their own resistance to change and their conviction that the group needs them to conform with its expectations. So those small steps aren't easy. (We'll discuss unilateral change in Chapter 6.)

For that reason, intentions to change need to be stated publicly, in the presence of the other parties who will be affected and whose reactions are going to affect the changing individual. If Tom, Dick, and Harry constitute the group, it is a positive step forward just to get Tom committed to make a small change. Even if Dick and Harry still maintain that they shouldn't have to change, their tacit acceptance of Tom's commitment will at least reduce the obstacles to Tom's changing his own behavior.

> Changes that are consciously, explicitly acknowledged are easier to make, easier to cope with, and easier to retain.

There is no substitute for openly discussing how hard it feels to change: before anyone has expressed a willingness to try, then again at the time some individuals begin to talk about doing so, then as a way of cementing their intention and commitment to behave more constructively, and finally, as follow-up evaluation and reinforcement for whatever change does occur.

Springing the Finger Trap

The human tendency to point the finger of blame at others is a trap. Like the opposing digits caught in the child's novelty known as the Chinese finger trap, mutual blamers struggle hopelessly to escape. The technique I call "springing the finger trap" makes it crystal clear who is and who isn't prepared to shoulder some responsibility for changing their own behavior. What will they do differently, henceforth, in response to the stresses and fears that have triggered unproductive conflict in the past?

Use this technique in a meeting of all the people who are blaming each other. If there are n people involved, draw a large $n \times n$ chart with their names across the top and, in the same order, down the left side (Figure 4-1). Make it clear that each column represents one person's opinions and that each row represents changes the group would like to see in one person's behavior. In this example, suppose Anne, Bob, Carl, and Doug represent the principal antagonists in the contentious organization we visited in Chapters 2 and 3. The whole company has

Figure 4-1. Springing the finger trap.

	Anne says:	Bob says:	Carl says:	Doug says:
Anne change:	**?**	stop seeing Bob as enemy	stop being paranoid	cut out power struggle with Doug
Bob change:	end male chauvinism end animosity toward Anne move his office	**?**		end animosity toward Anne
Carl change:	end male chauvinism take more initiative		**?**	wake up and look beyond organization chart
Doug change:	end male chauvinism		stop usurping authority	cut out power struggle with Anne

heard too many complaints by and about the members of this supposed team, including various ultimatums. "Either she goes or I go," Bob has said about Anne. "I can't work with her."

The company has sent you to help the antagonists get out of that rut. In one of your first meetings, you announce that they need to fill in this chart. Anne's column ("Anne says") represents Anne's opinions. Bob doesn't agree with her opinion that the problem would be solved if he moved to another floor or building. But Bob and Anne don't need to argue about that. If he doesn't accept her analysis of the problem, he simply refuses to copy that sentence into his "Bob says Bob should change" cell on the diagonal.

Don't tell the group, at the start, that the diagonal cells are especially important. You'll be able to make that point more dramatically after filling in the whole chart. Take your time, first, and be sure you have asked about every cell. Don't be surprised if one or more cells on the main diagonal are left empty. Bob can't think of anything he needs to change about his own behavior. "I'm perfect," he jokes—and he doesn't mean exactly that, but he would like to believe that he's not at fault. If the others would just measure up, the problem would be solved.

When all are satisfied with their contributions and have had ample opportunity to comment on the whole chart, take a different-colored marker and outline the diagonal cells. "I'm sorry to tell you, folks, that these are the only cells where anything is going to happen." When I do this (I use such a chart sooner or later with just about every group I work with), I usually X out the other cells, saying, "Forget it!" and "This is baloney! There is only one person in the world you can change, and it's hard enough to make even a little change in that stubborn so-and-so. If Anne doesn't change Anne, no one else can. If Bob isn't going to change Bob. . . ." At best, what you have written in a cell like "Bob says Anne should change . . ." might be taken as suggestions for Anne to consider putting into her own cell on the diagonal. (Figure 4-2 shows how this technique fits into Plan C and your larger game plan.)

One might think anyone would now be embarrassed to

Figure 4-2. Plan C: Gain commitment to change.

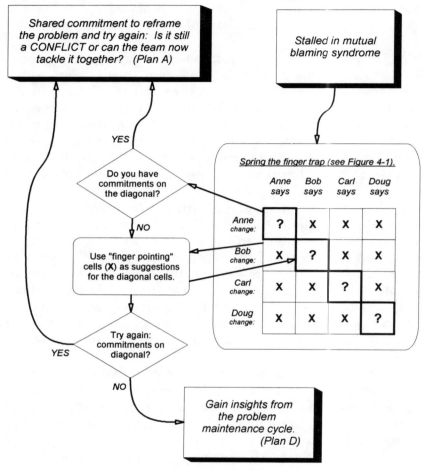

have blank cells on the diagonal (like Anne, Bob, and Carl in Figure 4-1). Under peer pressure, they could hardly refuse to take at least one of the group's suggestions and pledge themselves to make that change, or at least to think about working on it. Some will do so, perhaps modifying and reframing the suggestions, and those pledges should be taken as commitments, which we will discuss in a moment. However, some people will still refuse—perhaps defiantly—to acknowledge their own responsibility for either the problem or its solution. They may say, "I'm not going to do that until you show me you've stopped. . . ." Or, "You won't have to worry about that if you stay out of my. . . ."

If you can't sell certain individuals on committing themselves to change, don't press them any further. Rather, congratulate them for their honesty. They don't intend to change, and they don't want to create any false expectations. The truth is that they may change their mind at a later stage; but for now, it is better to leave them hanging there. They have isolated themselves.

What if the entire diagonal is blank? This happens frequently, especially in a 2 × 2 chart (two disputants). After all, if these folks were reasonable and sensible, they wouldn't be stuck in that quarrel in the first place, would they? I have had as large a group as father, son-in-law, and four sons leave all six cells on the main diagonal blank while filling in every one of the other thirty cells with mutual critiques and demands for change. (Try this at home, if you have bickering children.) In a case like that, don't be reluctant to say, "I'm sorry. I can't help you." And just wait.

Joining the Resistance

If IQ tests measured the ability to think of excuses, most of us would score in the genius category. As a change agent, you probably recognize many excuses as flimsy, fallacious, illogical, or dishonest. How far people let you challenge their bogus excuses is a measure of the strength of your relationship with them and of how well you balanced your joining with all factions of the conflict. No matter how successful you are at dismissing those excuses, though, you haven't removed their *reasons* for resistance: not always rational, but nonetheless real and compelling reasons. Sooner or later, the resistant individual or entire group expresses a candid fear or worry about what might happen if they were to accept the suggestion to change. (See Chapter 5 for a discussion of how you discover the secret basis of their resistance.)

We shall use a well-known sales technique called *joining the resistance,* which has many applications beyond the field of conflict resolution. The principle behind it is that people don't respond well to suggestions that dismiss the importance of whatever fears underlie their resistance. They respond very well to someone who shares or accepts the validity of their fears and offers to help address their concern.

Let's say someone has just made an adaptive suggestion and someone else has offered resistance based on poor reasoning (in your judgment). It doesn't matter whether you are the one who made the suggestion or just the facilitator of a discussion; this technique works the same either way.

Your first step is to clearly identify both the suggestion and the counterargument, using active listening to be sure you understand. Do *not* dismiss the counterargument as fallacious or insignificant.

Ellen's and George's different opinions about organizational priorities are sincere, but they are also aspects of a knee-jerk mutual opposition. On this occasion Ellen makes a good suggestion, but George argues against it. You don't say that you suspect he would have disagreed with her suggestion no matter what it was. Instead, you say, "So we understand that Ellen is arguing in favor of downsizing the department for reasons of cost control, but George is concerned about preserving our reputation for customer service."

Clarify the reason for the counterarguments. What is the resistant party trying to achieve, preserve, or avoid? Reframe that underlying motive as being essentially positive. It is *not resistance.* It is prudence, desire for growth, loyalty, passion for excellence, concern for people, or another worthwhile concern.

Make an extra joining gesture, if necessary, to put yourself on the side of the resistant party:

"I'm gonna move my chair over here and sit in George's corner."
Or (depending on the situation): "I appreciate your candor."
Or: "Thank you for raising that concern."

Now agree with the positive motive as you've reframed it, and justify the proposed constructive action as being *in line* with that motive:

"It seems to me Ellen's organizational scheme will really accomplish both goals, downsizing as well as personalizing our relations with customers, as George suggests."

A *salesperson*: "In fact, that's exactly what this product will do for you: save you money."

Notice how this technique moves the discussion back to the level of Plan A, with both parties looking for shared goals. You are still trying to get people to change their positions but on a win/win basis. It isn't a matter of helping Ellen convince George that he has been wrong. It is a matter of reframing the whole discussion so that both of them are right. Modify the original suggestion if necessary, and reframe it as the *product* of the resistant party's clarification of concerns.

"This is why it's so productive to brainstorm together, because what you've come up with is a better plan."

Finally, consolidate the step you have just taken toward consensus. Formalize a message or decision in the form of a contract, a written policy statement, or a dated memorandum. Sales people call this the closing. You might call it manipulative. I call it gaining commitment to change.

Harnessing the Commitment: Accentuate the Positive

Is change good or bad? We all say that it's inevitable and desirable; yet we naturally resist change in ourselves and more often resent than applaud it in others. Realizing that, many leaders try to sneak changes in the door by making them as subtle and imperceptible as possible. In fact, however, changes in people's relationships, trust, and respect for one another are unlikely to succeed unless those people dramatically declare and openly discuss their commitment to those changes.

Therefore you have everything to gain by positively labeling the conflict and congratulating the organization on its capacity to resolve it. Hence the name Conflict-Resolving System (CRS). Call it anything you want, so long as you make a big deal out of it. We'll return to that point in Chapter 7, but here we need to contrast negative versus positive ways of framing the same events and the same organizational characteristics. Figure 4-3 presents alternative ways of making the same point, through every stage of conflict resolution: identifying and labeling the problem, tracing the habitual cycle, expressing any shared fears that the group has avoided facing, describing old and new behavior, and specifying what each individual will be willing and able to change.

These examples are further applications of the principle of reframing (Chapters 2 and 3). Some of them may appear minor, simply a choice of rhetorical style. But as you practice, you will find that positive ways of making your points in conflictive situations go a long way. The more tense and irritated people are, and the more they align themselves with different positions, the more you risk antagonizing them by phrasing yourself as in the left-hand column of Figure 4-3 and the more effective you can be by showing respect as in the right-hand column.

Follow-Up

As with so much in life, follow-up is essential: coming together formally after an appropriate time has passed to evaluate the changes and decide whether the progress has been sufficient. The results of that assessment will determine your course of action, as suggested in Figure 4-2.

If the progress has been great, make a big deal out of it. Celebrate and give lavish praise where due. Your organization is moving in the direction of making the CRS flowchart (Figure 1-1) your norm. We'll look at ways of institutionalizing CRS and capitalizing upon it in Chapter 7.

On the other hand, if there has been but little progress, repeat the processes of goal setting (Plan A), valuing differences (Plan B), and specifying individual commitments (this

Figure 4-3. Negative vs. positive framing.

Instead of framing events NEGATIVELY	**You can frame the same events POSITIVELY**

Identifying and labeling the problem:

We have some idiots in this outfit who only think of themselves.	We're working on greater sensitivity to one another's needs.

Tracing the habitual cycle:

Every time I take some initiative, you act like I'm invading your turf and you go out of your way to nitpick ...	When my attempts at initiative seem to rub you the wrong way, and you then critique what I've done, my reaction is ...

Expressing the shared fears:

We're scared little babies, really, ...	We all share a concern about what might happen if ...
You're all walking around afraid to breathe lest you give Fred a heart attack.	Because you care about Fred's health, ...

Describing old and new behavior:

The slightest implication that anyone might be dissatisfied <u>drives</u> her ...	The inability to make everyone happy <u>drove</u> her ... (use the past tense rather than the present tense to describe what you hope will now change)
So I'm supposed to ...	So what I now do is ...

Specifying what each individual will change:

Fine, I'll let them continue as always, since there's nothing I can do about it.	The part of it I can control is my own reaction if and when that continues to happen. I'll work on ....
Don't blame me, then, the next time they	Please let me know the next time I come across to you as arrogant or disrespectful, because I'm sure it's going to take me a while to change and I'll need your help.

chapter). The only constraints on the number of trips you may make around the loop are people's patience and alliance with you.

What if you haven't made any progress at all? It may be that participants gave no more than lip service to their commitments to change. Their actions continue to belie their words. Good; now you have confirmed that. If you were using Plan C to test what I called "individual issues" in Chapter 3, then you can now choose from among the three "give up" options: presenting an ultimatum, removing the offender, or removing yourself.

The final possibility, which is difficult to admit but perhaps the most likely explanation, is that you haven't understood the problem in the first place. It may even appear to have been solved for a while, but then it comes back in another version. "There they go again," group members or outsiders say of the principals, "another round of the title bout."

Those cases require us to go a little deeper into the dynamics of conflicts within groups. Chapter 5 introduces the concept of the sustained conflict cycle.

5

Plan D: Analyze the Recurring Cycle

Plan D addresses the most distinctive feature of within-group conflicts as compared to those between people who neither work nor live together. The serious, chronic conflicts within groups follow a cyclic pattern. The particular battle of the day is only a symptom of underlying tensions, which flare up, subside for a while, blow up again. Peace is restored, then lost in yet another skirmish. We must understand and address the dynamic tensions that drive that recurring cycle if we hope to improve the parties' working relationships in any lasting way.

Why Communication Is Not Enough

You arrive at this section of the Conflict-Resolving System (CRS) flowchart when conflict keeps recurring despite your efforts at Plans A, B, and C. Therefore we'll now focus on that recurring cycle (Figure 5-1) and on a profound truth about it: *The reason it keeps coming back around again is that people are not really fighting about what they say they are fighting about.*

Any two people who come into contact, even complete strangers, immediately begin to affect one another. But in a group of individuals who have a working relationship (as in a family), the mutual effects are so powerful and enduring that group members come to share a whole set of fears, apprehensions, and distortions. In Chapter 3 we looked at individual misapprehensions that are due, basically, to not knowing other people well enough. Now we're saying, in addition, that within

Figure 5-1. The cycle of recurring conflict.

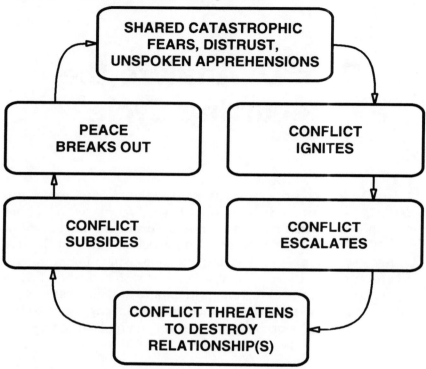

a relationship of any kind, members' shared history gives them *shared* apprehensions over and above their differences. In other words, when the same pattern of conflict recurs again and again in a group, it is probably due to knowing each other too well.

Figure 5-2 illustrates the cycle of sustained conflict in a married couple, George and Martha in *Who's Afraid of Virginia Woolf?* Edward Albee's play portrays an excruciating pattern of pain-to-avoid-pain, which George and Martha have sustained for more than twenty years. They lacerate one another with humiliating insults, mercilessly, until it seems they could not possibly stay together. Then one of them makes a wisecrack (at one point, George suddenly aims a pistol at Martha's head and pulls the trigger, only to release a little flag that says "Bang!"),

Figure 5-2. The cycle of recurring conflict in *Who's Afraid of Virginia Woolf?* by Edward Albee.

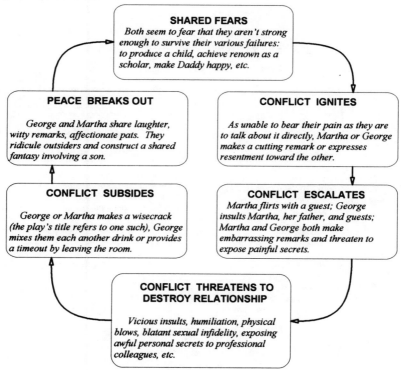

provoking affectionate laughter and a temporary cease-fire. But that soon becomes uncomfortable and intolerable because of the emptiness and unresolved grief in their childless marriage. They avoid facing their grief by stirring up the more familiar, controllable pain of mutual verbal abuse, Martha's debauchery, and George's cruelty to her invited guests.

Subtler cycles occur in business organizations. To see them, you need to know how to analyze a conflict in terms of those six phases of the cycle. You'll do this every time you encounter a recurring conflict that isn't resolved by clarifying shared goals, searching for win/win solutions, and valuing differences. Ask the analytic questions in Figure 5-3. You can ask the whole group to help you fill in the answers to those ques-

Figure 5-3. Plan D: Analyze the recurring cycle.

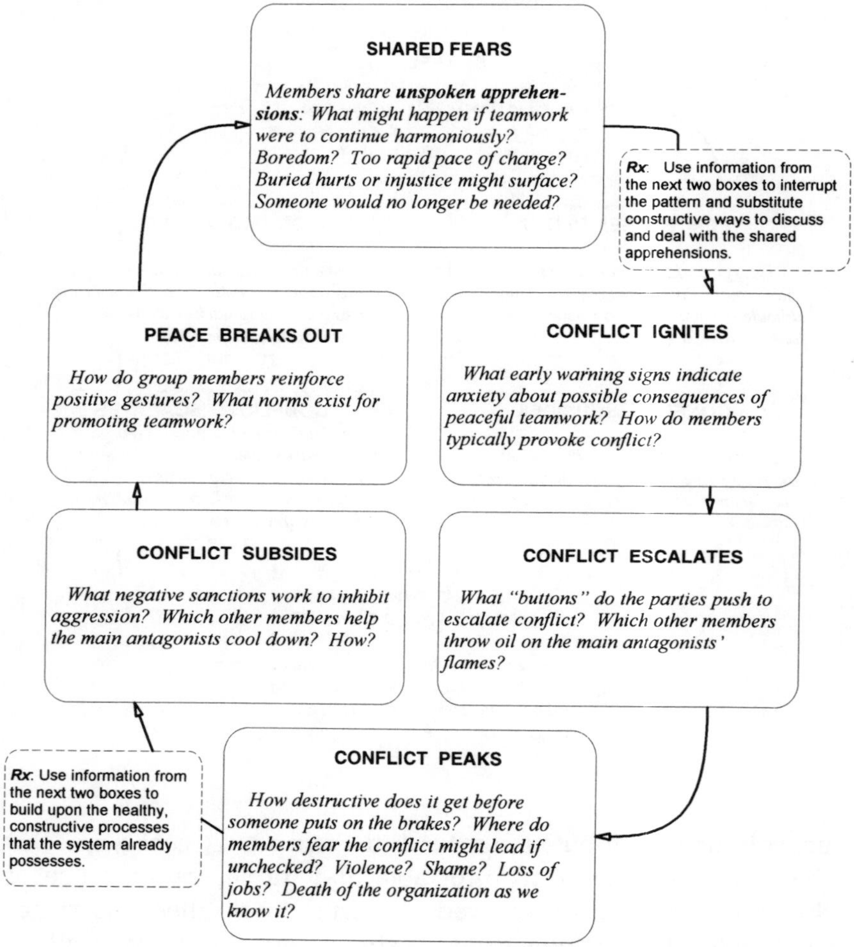

SHARED FEARS

*Members share **unspoken apprehensions**: What might happen if teamwork were to continue harmoniously? Boredom? Too rapid pace of change? Buried hurts or injustice might surface? Someone would no longer be needed?*

Rx. Use information from the next two boxes to interrupt the pattern and substitute constructive ways to discuss and deal with the shared apprehensions.

PEACE BREAKS OUT

How do group members reinforce positive gestures? What norms exist for promoting teamwork?

CONFLICT IGNITES

What early warning signs indicate anxiety about possible consequences of peaceful teamwork? How do members typically provoke conflict?

CONFLICT SUBSIDES

What negative sanctions work to inhibit aggression? Which other members help the main antagonists cool down? How?

CONFLICT ESCALATES

What "buttons" do the parties push to escalate conflict? Which other members throw oil on the main antagonists' flames?

Rx. Use information from the next two boxes to build upon the healthy, constructive processes that the system already possesses.

CONFLICT PEAKS

How destructive does it get before someone puts on the brakes? Where do members fear the conflict might lead if unchecked? Violence? Shame? Loss of jobs? Death of the organization as we know it?

tions (start with a similar chart with the six boxes blank). Or you can just chart the cycle privately for your own use.

Later in this chapter I show you how to use this information as a change agent; first, however, some practical suggestions about gathering the data. Plan D is really a technique for getting below the surface explanations of what people *say* they are fighting about and even what they *think* they are fighting about, to social-dynamic reasons, which they haven't thought much about. (Like it or not, you are about to enter the world of the psychological detective.)

To fill in the boxes, you can start wherever the most obvious data are. For example, if the clearest observation is that accusations of selfishness invariably push someone's rage button, you might work your way both forward and backward from Conflict Ignites. What usually provokes that kind of accusation in the first place? What kind of reaction does it provoke? Counteraccusations? How far does the rage go? Who fans the flames (Conflict Escalates)? How hot do they get and how long do members tolerate them (Conflict Peaks) before hauling out the fire brigade? What extinguishes the flames (Conflict Subsides)?

Your task is to fill in the whole chart. As you move clockwise around the circle to Peace Breaks Out, if you can't learn why the peace changes from a relief to a renewed source of anxiety, jump to Conflict Ignites and work backward to Shared Fears. What are those fears? Your initial discussion may yield only a hint or a first approximation. It may take more than one interview; keep at it.

This circular method belongs to the consulting approach known as "process research." You are challenging the participants' resistance to change in order to understand their process and to find out how you can help them improve it. With practice, the technique will become second nature. Let's look at some business organization examples and theorize a little about why this pattern is so universal.

Why Groups, Left to Themselves, Usually Maintain Conflict

Conflict is costly and painful. Why, then, is it so popular—even among folks who care about one another and have everything to gain by working together in harmony? The best answer psychologists have been able to discover is that members of a group *are* working together when they engage in repetitive, predictable dispute cycles. They are *collaborating to avoid something worse.*

It will be clearest to begin with a family business, after which we'll see how the same cycles of sustained conflict arise in nonfamily organizations.

Mel's two sons, ages 26 and 29, work with him in a retail chain of twelve furniture stores. His younger son has been working in the business nearly six years, ever since deciding that college was not for him. Mel attributes most of the company's growth, in fact, to that son's efforts. His older son only joined them two years ago, having worked on information systems at Wal-Mart Corporation for four years after taking a degree in computer sciences.

With one brother's knowledge of the furniture business and the other's sophistication about the aggressive use of information systems in a multilocation business, it ought to be an excellent team. But guess what? They fight constantly, usually over petty matters like who failed to record something, or lost a file, or forgot to give the other a telephone message, or okayed an employee's leaving early.

Mel is sure "the business needs both boys' talents." Nonetheless, instead of helping them ease up on each other, he finds himself constantly scrapping with whichever one is currently complaining the loudest. They shout, hurl epithets, and ridicule each other to employees. If he doesn't hear about it from another manager, Mel will hear sooner or later from his younger son, who keeps yelling about his "seniority" and claims not to know what his brother does all day. Depending on the story, Mel then yells at the older or the younger son or both, and they scream louder at him, making matters worse.

In this case, Mel and his sons may spend most of their time—most days and most hours of the day—somewhere between Conflict Ignites and Conflict Peaks. As unpleasant as their fights appear to others, only infrequently does the fighting grow intolerable to the fighters themselves. When that does happen, they ease off, but they don't tarry long in a truce before working their way around to the next conflagration.

We all know groups that are just the opposite: so averse to conflict that it takes almost no time for them to get to Conflict Subsides and then a long time before revisiting Conflict Ignites.

In fact, they may hit what for them is a peak, triggering pacification behavior almost before an outsider is able to discern that they clashed. Then they remain in apparent peace and harmony for weeks or months recovering from the shock, before the next conflict.

Notice that both extreme cases, the one seeming to fight all the time and the other barely seeming to fight at all, exhibit the same circular pattern. The question that haunts us, as reasonable observers, is why they don't stay in Peace. Where do those apprehensions come from, just when things ought to be copacetic? And when they do arise, why do they trigger the same old battle instead of a nice, reasonable discussion?

In other words, *why does peace lead to conflict?* It isn't that people just love to fight. It happens for either of two reasons:

1. Sometimes, what looks like peace isn't really peace. The true conflict hasn't been discussed, let alone successfully resolved, and everyone knows it—unconsciously if not consciously. They collaborate to keep fighting about trivia in hopes of getting to the real issues, but when it gets too dangerous they back away without having done so. The ensuing cease-fire reduces the danger or dulls their memory of how frightening the heat of battle was. Then they are willing to take up their weapons again.

2. Alternatively, the peace itself is dangerous. Even if some earlier issues did get resolved, that very fact raises new questions the collaborators sense they aren't ready to face. For example: If we are working well together, does that mean one of us is capable of being the organization's next president? Which one of us? Or: If we are functioning more productively as a team, does that mean some of us aren't needed anymore?

In either case, the antagonists are fighting as an ineffective way of solving a problem. Your job is to offer them a more effective way of solving it or at least empower them to talk about it so they can find the solution themselves.

As you work on analyzing a cycle of sustained conflict (Figure 5-3), it often helps to ask the parties a radical question: "What are you fighting together to avoid?"

What a strange suggestion! Mel's two sons, for example, think they are fighting *against* each other to achieve incompatible goals. It is counterintuitive to suggest that they are actually working together to maintain the fight in order to avoid some state of affairs that they both sense would be worse than the cost of their struggle. Yet planting that suggestion almost always bears fruit.

In fact, it's fruitless to try to help resolve a conflict without asking the parties (and/or asking ourselves) this question. Here is another way to word it: "What do you think might happen if you didn't do what you usually do in that situation?" What if, for example, you gave each other the benefit of the doubt and treated each other like clients? That question usually brings to light the real force behind the conflict, the combatants' real apprehensions, which could be anything from "if I let her get away with that, she'd walk all over me" to "the boss wouldn't have anything to bitch about" to "we wouldn't need as many workers" to "we wouldn't have any excuses for failure." Any of those would be a more productive way to frame the problem than their list of mutual grievances, accusations, and attacks.

The "What Might Happen If . . . ?" Question

What do you think might happen if you didn't do what you usually do in that situation?

The combatants in a sustained conflict cycle are aware of these apprehensions but not aware that they've been fighting to protect the whole system from having to face and deal with them. Until the group does face those issues, any peace will be illusory, only a temporary cease-fire.

The "What might happen if . . . ?" question bypasses the excuses people prefer to use when justifying aggressive or defensive positions. In the example of Mel's furniture chain, what might happen if the sons were to stop attacking and undermining each other over petty matters? Chances are, they might agree on the need to make changes, which would soon progress too rapidly for their father's comfort. Deep down, they don't believe he really wants them to take over. Deep down, they aren't sure they are capable of making those decisions. And they are collaborating to make sure Dad doesn't leave. They don't enjoy squabbling with one another, but the alternatives are too frightening to think about. It is easier to point the finger of blame at a brother than to dwell on doubts about one's own competence.

Let us not stop with the sons' motives. Does Mel really want them to feel competent? What would happen to his own self-esteem if their judgment turned out to be as good as or better than his? *His self-esteem depends on pointing to their inadequacies.* This is not just a matter of the difficulty any entrepreneur has letting go of his "baby," the business he has nurtured for thirty years. It isn't easy in any case, but the two young men probably would not be fighting so valiantly to prove they can't get along without him if Dad had done a good job of building up their self-confidence from childhood on. We generally find mutual envy and enmity among adult siblings in a business only when they have suffered from excessive rivalry all their lives—before they ever came to work for their father—fighting for the approval he didn't know how to give his children.

We began with a family business example because cycles of sustained conflict are so prevalent in family systems. In fact, conflict resolution and team building with family firms almost *always* entail Plan D. However, such problem cycles also arise in every kind of organization.

The following two examples show how the excuses people give for their sustained battles often have little connection to the shared unconscious motives that would remain unspoken if no one were to ask the radical question, "What would happen if . . . ?"

Empire Realty was a medium-size property management firm in a region with an alarmingly high office vacancy rate. A group of executives headed by Rick and Gino had recently acquired the company from its retiring owner. Rick, with the title of president, was in charge of selling Empire's services to property owners. Gino supervised their five offices. Their conflict had begun when Rick accused Gino and his group of hiding information from him and of carelessly losing tenants.

Gino had a different slant on their failure to communicate. "Every time Rick blows a sale, he looks for someone to blame."

"What would happen if you two weren't arguing over who screwed up?" I asked.

I had to repeat the question a couple of times, but finally Gino replied, "The only way we wouldn't argue about that is if we were not, in fact, screwing up."

"What would be wrong with that?"

They looked puzzled. "Nothing would be *wrong* with it," Gino said. "That's what we're seeking."

"No, you really aren't," I challenged him. "You're each spending half your energy demanding that the other guy do the changing and half your energy giving him excuses not to. So I guess one thing you're trying to do is keep on having this argument." This elicited a smile, indicating that I might be on the right track. I continued, "What can you imagine as a possible negative if the whole problem were to go away, in favor of smooth, productive communication?"

"I can tell you one thing," Rick volunteered. "We'd probably start asking ourselves if we're in the wrong business." He said this as if he were joking, but it turned out that he was not. I learned that both men were terrified about the debt they had incurred to acquire what might possibly be a dying business. They were so far from having any ideas about redirecting the business that they had avoided voicing their fears to anyone, even their wives. And the principal way they had avoided doing that was to fuss and fume about one another's incompetence and possible dishonesty.

My only contribution based on that discovery was to help Rick and Gino start talking, along with their partners and industry advisors, about the real problem. Here is the other example:

Ted is president of NetTech, a firm that provides software engineers and programmers to companies that are redesigning their information systems. The difference between the salaries of his two hundred employees and their fees billed to clients is Net-Tech's profit margin. Hence the monthly utilization reports from Cathy, the firm's controller, ought to provide vital information to branch managers (the very information, in fact, which will deter-mine their annual performance bonuses). Yet she complains that they never look at her reports, react with hostility when she urges them to use them, and refuse to make their office administrators cooperate in getting the needed data into her system accurately and on time.

Ted learns that a virtual state of war exists between Cathy and Ron, his vice president of sales (to whom all six branch managers report; see Figure 5-4). Ron accuses her of lying when she "comes crying to you with complaints of mistreatment." She blames Ron entirely for the disrespect she gets all the way down the line, at-

Figure 5-4. Organizational responsibility of NetTech Corporation officers.

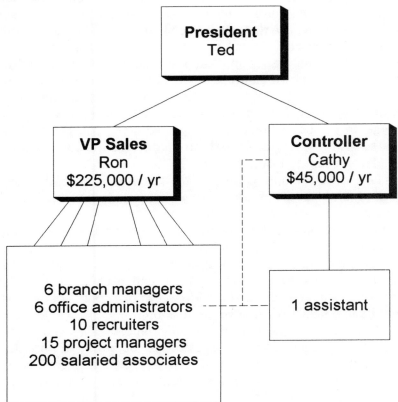

tributing about half of the problem to his sexism and half to defensiveness about his lack of management skill. (Twice, she got Ted to send Ron to AMA seminars and actually registered him, but he found last-minute excuses not to go.)

Ron, 43, who started his career as a programmer, came to this firm twelve years ago, managing three different branches before his recent promotion to the main office. Cathy, 28, was hired only four years ago as assistant to the controller. She immediately began to campaign for using the firm's expertise to revamp their own system. Her boss retired and she got his job, although not his full salary. Ron accuses her of trying to usurp his authority, treating the branch managers (all men) arrogantly and their administrators (all women) as her subordinates.

Ted has already asked Ron to take Cathy to lunch and resolve their differences without involving him. That didn't help. When Ted realizes that he will have to mediate, he tries Plan A. It only takes five minutes to realize that will go nowhere. Plan B helps to clarify the issue of male chauvinism, which Ron acknowledges (though he feels some of the branch managers are guiltier than he, and he claims that the female administrators have no problems with the guys and can't stand Cathy). Ted tries "springing the finger trap" (Figure 4-1), including himself as one of the parties who need to change. In the box labeled "Ted says Ted must change . . . ," he pointedly writes, "Be clearer about who's responsible for what" and "Don't seem to take sides."

Ron takes the hint, committing himself to "Give Cathy more support" and "Don't assume Cathy's intentions are malicious." Cathy can think of nothing to write under "Cathy says Cathy should change . . . ," rejecting the two men's suggestions. Before giving up on her, however, Ted decides to try Plan D.

"This dispute keeps going around and around," he says. "You get into a knock-down, drag-out fight, call each other a lot of names, and then it subsides for a few weeks or a couple of months. What happens? Why does it come up again?"

Cathy and Ron each offer one-sided accounts of what starts their trouble. "Let's assume you're both collaborating in this," Ted says. "Let's assume there's a hidden payoff in this conflict, or maybe a hidden cost when you get along. After all, you both know very well how to push each other's buttons, and conversely, how to deal with each other professionally when you want to."

Cathy and Ron both look thoughtful, but they're not sure they understand where Ted is going. He tries the "What would happen if . . . ?" question: "What would happen if you two could trust each other and if you felt respected by each other? What would be wrong with working as a team?"

"What would *you* do?" Cathy asks.

"What do you mean?"

"Right now, a big part of your job is mediating between the two of us. You're trying to spend less of your time on day-to-day operations, which is good, but maybe if you didn't have this problem to deal with frequently, you might get a little *too far* away from things."

That turns out to be the first thing Cathy has ever said that Ron can fully agree with. "I'd put it a little differently, maybe," he says. "I think between the two of us we *should* be handling all the day-to-day stuff. I should only involve you in meeting with key clients and certain new prospects; Cathy should involve you with the bank, stuff like that. But maybe we don't have the confidence that the two of us *can* essentially run the company together. We can be professional and cordial with each other when we want to be. But if she doesn't have confidence that I really know what I'm doing, and if I don't think she has any knowledge at all of what we on the line do, then we aren't ready to have you withdraw to a chairman-of-the-board-type role."

Ted has been a collaborator in maintaining the problem by his failure to clarify Cathy's job to Ron and by habitually trying to pacify both of them by agreeing when they denigrate one another. In truth, he has been ambivalent about the changes in his own role that the company's growth and development necessitate.

Figure 5-5 summarizes the analysis of this sustained conflict cycle. Instead of arguing forever about their excuses for fighting, they can now turn their attention to the matters they were fighting to avoid.

Figure 5-5. The cycle of recurring conflict as shown by NetTech's president and two key executives.

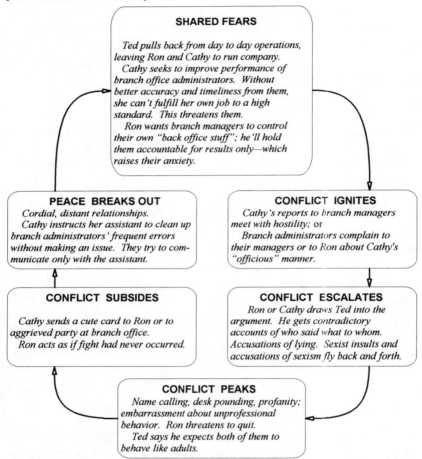

The Change Agent's Challenge

In the Empire Realty case, my work was essentially done when I helped Rick and Gino gain insights about what they were fighting together to avoid talking about. In the last example, Ted's, Cathy's, and Ron's insights were only the beginning of a team-building process that would be a key part of their organizational change. When you are called upon to improve a set of relationships, how can you use Plan D insights to direct the change process?

Recall that in Plans A and B we tried to resolve the conflict through better listening and problem solving based on what the disputants said they were fighting about. When Plans A and B fail, it means the disputants aren't saying or maybe are not even aware of what the real fight is about. However, this does not mean that once made aware of it, they can just cut it out.

Unlike conflicts between strangers, which can often be settled by correcting their misunderstandings and negotiating a compromise, conflicts between members of the same group may be based on a very good understanding and, in fact, an unspoken compact: "Let's you and me fight." Their conflict will subside when its purpose seems to have been served, but then it is only a matter of time before the system gets out of equilibrium again because the real problem was never addressed. So the members will fall back upon their habits of pushing the familiar buttons to get the familiar result. Therefore, for anyone who hopes to move them off that merry-go-round (whether you're one of the disputants yourself, their supervisor, another member of the organization, or a professional consultant), the challenge is usually greater than just talking the parties into stopping their destructive behavior (Plan C). You have to help them find better ways of dealing with their underlying apprehensions.

> The mutually destructive pattern of fighting will continue until someone gives the parties a more straightforward way to deal with whatever issue they've been fighting to avoid.

The remainder of this chapter details four steps for helping people face whatever issue they've been avoiding:

1. *Identify the individual fears and shared apprehensions* that trigger conflict and alienation.
2. Help the parties themselves *learn to recognize* and even

anticipate that those apprehensions will lead to another round of "here we go again," unless they consciously choose to respond more constructively.

3. Help them *learn to interrupt the process* of mutual button pushing that typically escalates their conflict.

4. *Help members continue to use their existing ways* of making peace (already in their repertoires), reinforcing them to use those behaviors sooner.

Let's see how those steps might help the leaders of a large nonprofit organization.

Barb and Karen were among the founders of Greensleeves more than a decade ago. Barb has recently been elected president, and Karen continues as first vice president of the organization. Karen doesn't like the imperious way Barb has begun to exercise her authority, and Barb regards Karen as a threat to her presidency, but they also share many concerns and a sense that conflict between them could endanger the cohesiveness and equilibrium of their organization. A delicate balance keeps them functioning together. That balance is upset when, for example, Karen takes offense at a perceived slight without giving Barb a chance to realize how her action affected Karen and to clarify her nonhostile intentions. As other officers and board members are drawn in, both women see in one another's reactions the confirmation of their worst fears. Their separate apprehensions of one another, in other words, magnify and rigidify all differences in their positions. Their concerns, desires, and views of reality interact in a conflict-escalating way.

Soon, the escalating conflict triggers anxiety among the leadership. The fear of what a full-blown battle would mean to their relationship or to the organization as a whole stops them from going too far. Others intervene by reminding Karen and Barb of their shared mission. (They move clockwise from Conflict Peaks to Conflict Subsides in Figure 5-6.) As peace returns, those other leaders reinforce Karen's and Barb's cooperative words and actions. All is harmony again.

Unfortunately, the mistrustful rivalry between Karen and Barb wasn't addressed. Therefore as soon as it no longer threatens the

Figure 5-6. The cycle of recurring conflict as shown by the founders of a nonprofit organization.

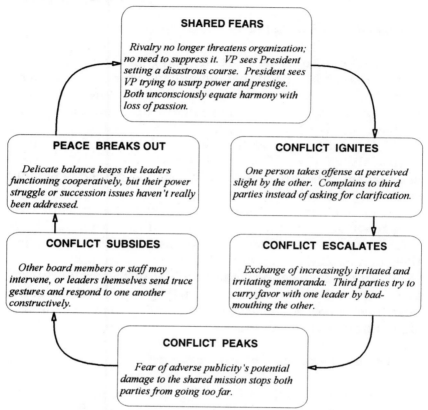

organization, they lose their motive to join in suppressing that rivalry. The peaceful coexistence rekindles their apprehensions: Karen thinks Barb is setting the organization on a disastrous course; Barb thinks Karen is trying to usurp her power and prestige. Furthermore, both share a fear (perhaps subconscious) that if it weren't for their power struggle, something even worse might happen. Loss of passion among the leadership? Deviation from the moderate policies that result from their balance of forces? Whatever their shared apprehension may be, when things get uncomfortably quiet, someone ignites another round of conflict, which escalates, and "There they go again." Thus their social system maintains an equilibrium, avoids change, and even avoids *thinking* about change.

Identify the Shared Fears

We have filled in the chart, spending plenty of time on the Shared Fears box. The "What might happen if . . . ?" question helped us discover Karen's and Barb's individual fears and misunderstandings, as well as some shared apprehensions. What we have now is a theory, which most of the participants seem to think has possible validity. But are the leaders' apprehensions realistic? *Would* Karen try to undermine Barb if she were less vigilant? *Would* Barb modify longstanding policies without consulting the board?

If people agree that those are realistic concerns, then we have redefined the problem. Go back to Plans B and C (Figure 5-7). Karen and Barb have been fighting for good reasons, and they aren't going to stop until circumstances change.

On the other hand, if their mutual distrust is unrealistic and their conflict unproductive, then they need to watch for the next time it occurs and try communicating better at the first sign of trouble (Plans C and A).

Learn to Recognize the Warning Signs

In the Conflict Ignites box of Figure 5-6 (as in 5-2, 5-3, and 5-5), the facilitator assembles a list of gestures and feelings that frequently get these people into trouble. The earlier they can recognize those, the better their chances of interrupting the cycle.

Learn What "Buttons" Typically Escalate the Conflict

The change agent who will be in the best position to highlight this sequence and coach people to anticipate the cycle and redirect it is the one who sits with them in actual meetings where the conflict has typically flared. That doesn't happen at retreats that emphasize irrelevant exercises, such as rope

Figure 5-7. After analyzing the cycle—what next?

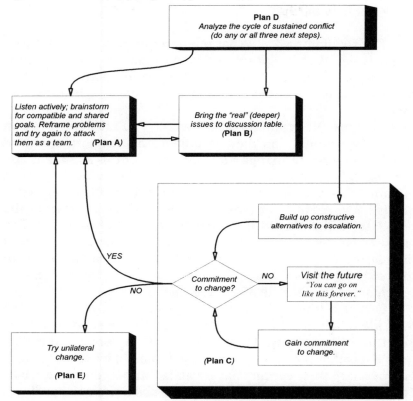

courses and artificial team problem solving. Such exercises present personal challenges to the individual members. They may also generate insights about group process in general and even elicit the group's habitual sequence of miscommunication and conflict; but they don't create an opportunity to revise that sequence as it applies to their normal work processes, so they can transfer what they are coached to do, back into the everyday setting. With the latter goal in mind, I strongly recommend—whether you are facilitating a retreat or consulting at the team's place of business—to have them conduct real meetings on real tasks, rather than simulation exercises.

Use the Peacemaking Instincts That Are
Already in the System

The facilitator asks "What might happen if . . . ?" the conflict between Barb and Karen were to escalate without pacification. He learns that the leaders share a commitment to maintain the organization's public image. Good. That is a healthy motive.

Who are the group members who try to make peace? Can they do so earlier? Can they become agents for permanent instead of temporary change? You can think of this as harnessing the system's habitual ways of reducing conflict when it gets out of hand. You can also visualize it as pushing those constructive habits back, counterclockwise, so that they become part of the response to the shared apprehensions in the first place. *Formerly, certain warning signs triggered conflict. In the future, we want those same warning signs to trigger constructive communication*—not to avoid the conflict, but to reframe it as soon as possible, as a problem for the team to attack together.

Let me put this concept another way. What you see on the left side of Figure 5-6 is evidence that this system has in its repertoire the skills we talked about in Chapters 2 and 3. The problem is that the people aren't used to mobilizing those skills except when their conflict has escalated into a terrifying crisis. Our job is to get them to exercise those skills *before* the problem becomes a crisis.

The best way to break bad habits is to build up the strength of other habits that are incompatible with them. Obviously it is easier to build strengths that already exist in the system than to introduce new behavior. Unfortunately, groups that are engaged in team building tend to concentrate on what is wrong with their current behavior and what is lacking. It takes a little more creativity to focus on their existing strengths and think about amplifying them. Yet that is actually the more promising approach.[1]

Along the same lines, review the section Joining the Resistance in Chapter 4. Your job is not to go head-to-head with people's fear of taking risks. Their resistance is too strong for you to talk them out of it directly. Be sure they know that you know they've had good reasons for maintaining the cycle of sustained conflict up to now. But for those same good reasons you're supporting them to try a more promising approach.

Returning to the Problem

Now the team takes those insights back to Plan A and tries to attack the real problem together. As Figure 5-7 indicates, they may revisit Plans B and C, too. Most of the people with whom you achieve insights about their sustained conflict cycles will be people whose mental health is relatively good and who aren't overly defensive. Now they realize that they can talk about the unthinkable or that their whole group shares the same worries and a commitment to avoid the same catastrophes. Often that is all they need in order to break their gridlock and begin to get things done.

Don't underestimate the motivational power of your merely pointing out what people have been doing and telling them it will not work. "You can go on forever," you say, "alternating between the brink of warfare and the depths of denial; the real problem that you've been avoiding won't go away." (This is an elaboration of what you told them in Plan C.)

However, it may not be that easy to gain the commitment of everyone concerned, to change their pattern. Even with some acknowledgment of what leads to what in the recurring cycle of their conflict, suppose some or all of the members still maintain that they are not at fault. It is the other person's fault. "You want to know what would happen if I were to stop making those remarks or taking those evasive actions? Then *she* would. . . ."

Check that out with the other person. If the reply is, "No, I promise I won't; try me," that's great. Cajole the negative member into giving her a chance.

Unfortunately, the accused might reply instead, "You bet that's what I'd do, because I know you always. . . ." Pointing the finger of blame and thereby handicapping herself as the accuser's helpless victim, she is using the lack of change in others as an excuse for dancing to the same old tune. Once the group has identified more adaptive ways to function, everyone must decide who needs to change which behavior to make it better. So you return to the exercise "springing the finger trap" (Chapter 4) and get everyone to look at themselves instead of waiting for others to make the first moves.

The examples in this chapter have assumed an interviewer or facilitator who isn't a direct party to the conflict (except Ted—but even he thought at first he was only mediating a dispute between Ron and Cathy). It is always harder to see patterns when you are immersed in them. However, you can use these techniques to diagram and alter a sustained conflict cycle in your own relationships. And you can use the information gained thereby, to push the constructive processes back in time until they displace the habitual button pushing and flame fanning.

Let's say you are the enlightened member of a conflictive system; unfortunately, the only enlightened member. If you get nowhere, should you give up? Not until after trying Plan E, unilateral change—otherwise known as leadership.

Note

1. For an extended discussion of this and other topics that are only touched upon in the remaining chapters of this book, see Edgar Schein, *Organizational Culture and Leadership*, 2nd ed. (San Francisco: Jossey-Bass, 1992).

6

Plan E: Unilaterally Demonstrate Change

Suppose the other members of your group aren't willing to change. There may be one particular person you can't seem to work with and can't do anything about. Or perhaps your whole group keeps butting heads. Some of them have outright refused to change. Others gave lip service to a desire to improve teamwork, and, in response to peer pressure, acknowledged their own contributions to the problem. They expressed a willingness to "try" to change whatever part of the interaction is under their control, but somehow that never happened. They are waiting for other people to change first.

Everything we've said thus far indicates that it takes general goodwill and cooperation to change an organization from a problem-maintaining system into a problem-solving system. Nonetheless, a single individual can do much to stimulate positive change within an organization. And that doesn't just apply to those who are currently in leadership positions. In fact, Plan E can be an effective way to increase one's influence and status within the organization.

Bruce was one of four vice presidents reporting to a senior vice president at a large international corporation. His boss reported to the president of the North American division. Figure 6-1 (top half) shows the functional organization of those people Bruce dealt with directly, soon after a major change in their business vision and the firing of a senior vice president (position C).

The rapidity of change in this company had stirred up considerable fear, internal competitiveness, turfism, and resistance to

Figure 6-1. Functional organization of Bruce's corporation.

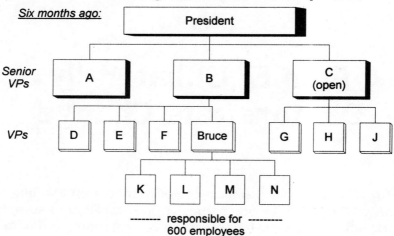

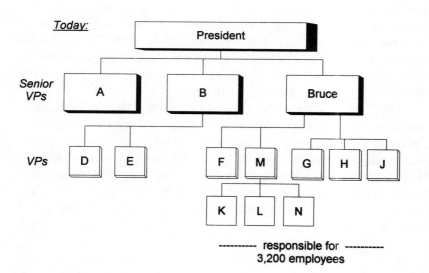

further change. The two individuals who occupied positions A and B, distrustful and antagonistic toward one another, didn't communicate well. The seven people at Bruce's level didn't function as teams because, in addition to the anxiety that pervaded the whole organization, some of them were jockeying for position C.

Six months later, Bruce was promoted to that position, also retaining his own team (one of whom became a vice president) and another group which had previously reported to B (see bottom half of Figure 6-1). He attributed this success to his one-man campaign for teamwork.

I had an opportunity to interview Bruce in the course of a subsequent team-building assignment for his company. It came as no surprise to learn that Bruce had essentially been applying Plan E. Based on sound management practices, good people skills, and considerable reading, he had applied the following principles:

❑ "I wrote out my philosophy of teamwork, basically that I take responsibility for doing my job in the way that anticipates everyone else's needs for information or involvement or whatever and doesn't slow anyone else down. I showed it to the people who reported to me, but mainly I just referred to it myself when deciding how I was going to handle something.

❑ "I told people in advance how I was going to make a decision or whatever, and then I almost always did it the way I said I would—or I got back to them and discussed the change. So, even if others were playing games with each other, I stayed out in the open: no surprises.

❑ "I don't expect others to be perfect team players, so I didn't overreact to petty stuff. I might express disappointment in someone's lack of cooperation or what seemed like troublemaking, but I didn't dwell on the negative.

❑ "I didn't lecture anyone else on teamwork. Other than telling my own people how we were going to relate to everyone else, I just practiced without preaching.

❑ "Whenever possible, I tried to anticipate in advance how I would probably feel pulled into infighting or turfism. Being prepared, I was usually able to put aside the instinctive reaction and stick with my program."

The result: Managers above, below, and on a par with Bruce learned that they could trust him to deal straight with them. The rivalry didn't stop with his promotion—in fact, he encountered some resentment on the part of everyone on the chart, except the president and M—but then he just continued to implement his unilateral plan. "You don't have to change," his behavior implied. "I'm going to play like a teammate of yours, regardless."

The more powerful an individual is at the outset, obviously, the faster he or she can motivate the whole system to change; yet it is also true for anyone at any level of the organization that leading its transformation into a problem-solving system can be a path to greater influence and power.

> "I alone am not powerful enough to change this system. But I'm not its victim; I control how the system affects me, how I present myself to others, and whether I continue to work in the organization or not."

Can one person change a system? Not alone, but change has to *start* with someone. More to the point, even if the system is more powerful than you alone, you don't have to be its victim. You control how you respond to the system, how you present yourself to others, and whether you continue to work in the organization. Those degrees of control are often enough to influence other members' attitudes toward positive changes; but when they don't, you haven't lost anything.

The Disarming Effect of Unilateral Disarmament

In this section, we'll assume that the dispute you're most concerned about is one in which you are a combatant—or, as you see it, a target of hostility. Naturally you feel the other parties are the aggressors and you are merely protecting yourself. The last thing that would come naturally to you under those circumstances would be to give up your counteroffensive weapons. The thought of unilateral disarmament always raises fears; you don't want to leave yourself vulnerable to attack. But remember that the other party is motivated by fear, too. When you become less threatening, you will have less to fear.

Pat, a production manager, and Henry, customer services manager, have a long-standing feud. Their boss tells them to cut it out and grow up; he's fed up with both of them. Pat decides to try unilateral disarmament.

"Henry," she says over lunch (her treat—and she says this no later than immediately after the waiter takes their order), "I want to speak more frankly and less defensively than I've ever done before. I have decided to take responsibility for anything and everything I can possibly do to make our working relationship productive." Then she goes on to explore with Henry what that might mean, unconditionally.

There are ways to disarm oneself dramatically while reducing the risks, no matter how aggressive your opponent may be:

- ❑ *Tell the world what to expect from you.* Then be sure your behavior is consistent with those expectations. No surprises.
- ❑ *Refer only to your own behavior,* avoiding the temptation to dwell on the (formerly) problematic behavior of others. Let bygones be bygones. (This principle is consistent with Plan A, focusing upon the shared goals rather than the differences.)
- ❑ *Don't demand instant appreciation and payback for every positive move you make.* Expect a lag before others' perceptions catch up with reality. (This corresponds to the POV understanding of Plan B.)
- ❑ Be prepared to *appreciate even tiny moves in the right direction* (as we do in Plan C); don't minimize them.
- ❑ Think about the system's reasons for resistance, and *provide healthier means to maintain equilibrium* (Plan D).

The Manager as Referee

Now let's look at a different situation, one in which you aren't one of the disputants. You are their manager. Two people who report to you keep coming to you with their complaints about one another. You are in the position of Ted, the company president I discussed in Chapter 5 (Figure 5-4), whose controller and vice president are at war with each other.

Ted has tried everything he can think of to get Cathy and Ron to work together more constructively except realizing that he owns the whole problem! Whatever he has been doing—listening patiently, shuttle diplomacy, telling them both they're right about the other's defects—has been maintaining the problem. Instead of trying to make nice to them (the more he does so, the more trouble they have with each other), what would happen if he did exactly the opposite: made life impossible for both of them until they solved the problem?

He says, "Cathy will quit if I stand up to her on this matter. I can't afford that; she's indispensable."

There are two faults with that reasoning; One is that you can't afford to keep an employee who has you over that kind of barrel. Furthermore, she won't quit. In fact, both people will be grateful that you broke their cycle of conflict. But you have to do it as outlined above, not just "Stop fighting or I'll punish both of you." How about asking the two of them to prepare a joint memo, which they both have to sign, addressing only those things they agree that you need to change about your own managerial style. However, this will only work if you (a) require them to do this task for you and (b) respond sincerely and visibly to their list of requested changes.

Ted doesn't think for a minute he's the whole problem or even the biggest problem. Cathy *is* defensive, never wrong, hostile. Ron *is* contemptuous of her, and sexist, and has poisoned the branch administrators against her, contrary to Ted's orders. But none of that has changed, so Ted asks himself—and them—what he can do unilaterally. He can see that he's been too conciliatory and supportive of each of them and knows it's true that he has tried to avoid conflict by allowing a great deal of vagueness in how he's defined Cathy's job. So he addresses himself to that, letting them know what he's doing and that he'll expect them to eliminate the problem once he takes care of his end of it.

The Volunteer Peacemaker: Risks and Rewards

The other situation in which you might act alone occurs when no one else is willing to take the lead in helping some members of your organization break the cycle of chronic conflict. You may be a human resources manager, called in when the line managers have thrown up their hands in despair. Or you may be a line manager: Your direct report asks for help, for example, with someone in the organization who's not subordinate to you.

The risks in such situations are two. One is that you put yourself into the middle of something that formerly "didn't involve you" (though of course it really does have an impact on everyone in the system). The second risk is that anything that upsets an equilibrium might cause even greater damage.

So how can you reduce the risks?

❑ Make your mandate explicit. Discuss with all sides the pros and cons of your getting involved. How will it affect their relationships with you? When does your involvement end? Can any of the parties (including yourself) terminate your involvement before that end is reached? How?

❑ Be prepared. What maneuvers can you expect on the basis of people's past behavior? How will you handle those moves? What might upset their fragile equilibrium? How will you respond to that?

❑ Prepare others: "We aren't eliminating your conflict; we're just trying to help you handle it a little more constructively in the future. It's inevitable that problems will continue to arise as we work on this. How will we deal with them?"

Although it is important to be mindful of those risks, the potential rewards of peacemaking are greater. Only one of those is the stake you have in improved relationships and better teamwork in your organization. Another is the fact that whatever real problems were being avoided through that constant or periodic sideshow are now going to be addressed for the first time in a straightforward way. Finally, there is the important fact that the organization members, including yourself, now recognize you as a leader.

7

Now We Are a Conflict-Resolving System

Our aspirations are higher than merely solving today's specific problem. Even if you came to this system hoping no more than to deal with a specific crisis, the payoff for your organization should consist of a significant change in the way its members view themselves. It's worth giving a name to their newly recognized capabilities: Conflict-Resolving System (CRS), which they can now apply to whatever future challenges demand excellence in communicating and in facilitating one another's work.

As a human resources manager for a large corporation, you oversee compensation, benefits, training, and recruiting for plants in three Canadian provinces. Your on-site human resources supervisor at one of those sites has a problem mediating a dispute between his new plant manager, Karen, and her purchasing manager, Marco. The latter happens to have been passed over for promotion when Karen was hired (though he denies this is an issue). They are barely on speaking terms, let alone working well together. You arrive, like the expert you are, to resolve their conflict.

What is your goal?

   a. To bring out their humanity and make them kinder, gentler, more fulfilled people?
   b. To improve their performance as a business team?
   c. To train them in better communication skills so you don't have to return to mediate their next dispute?

    d. To train their human resources manager so he can be more successful with these and all other employees?

    e. To change the culture of their plant, your whole region, and ultimately the entire corporation so that interpersonal problems are resolved as quickly and effectively as possible?

    f. To make the expectation that "we are good at resolving conflicts" a key element in the confidence and pride with which teams regard themselves throughout your company—part of what they see as their competitive edge and one reason they choose to work here?

The answer: all of the above. If you chose *b,* you were thinking only of your primary goal. But *a* is probably not incompatible with that; why not both *a* and *b*?

You might consider the next two answers, *c* and *d,* good secondary goals: to improve the disputants' communication skills and make their staff support person a better conflict resolver. If you can move in the direction of *c* and *d* while achieving *b,* so much the better. But are they only *secondary* goals? Think about it. It is Karen's and Marco's current dispute that is secondary: an acute symptom of a problem that will recur if you merely treat the symptom. Is it worth your going in just to put out that fire (goals *a* and *b*)? Or should you be there *primarily* to make a safety inspection and train the local fire station (goals *c* and *d*)? In general, doesn't a business organization need to view every significant problem as a possible recurring situation and therefore a case for continuous process improvement? The company that merely solves one problem after another, case by case, without improving its process for doing so—in effect, without a learning curve—is a company that fails to compete over time. This is no less true in the arena of internal communications than in manufacturing, marketing, or finance.

That brings us to *e* and *f,* goals that might strike some readers as grandiose. I would argue that *a* through *d* are merely necessary routine processes in running any organization. Any company that just stays alive will be addressing those goals continuously. To address them provides no competitive advantage. Only when you can influence your organizational culture (*e*), and particularly when members of the organization consciously regard their teamwork as a positive element in their identity (*f*), does it contribute sustainable advantage to your company.

This chapter shows how to leverage the systematic problem-solving processes we have outlined thus far, so the organization becomes not conflict free (which never happens, and we wouldn't want it) but *conflict transcendent*. Just as total quality management (TQM) is a constant, ongoing process with regard to a company's inputs and outputs, CRS is a constant aspect of excellence with regard to the way a company's human resources work together.

CRS as a Key Element of Team Building

Team building is a multifaceted process (Figure 7-1). Only one facet is Leadership, the personal qualities and management style of whoever builds and heads your team. Under the heading of Organization it includes finding the most productive

Figure 7-1. Facets of team building.

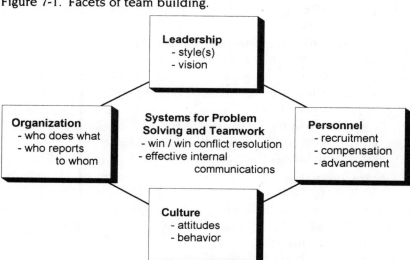

structure, job descriptions, and reporting relationships. Under the heading Personnel it includes recruitment, compensation, promotions, and employee development: getting the best people in the right jobs with effective incentives. And under the heading Culture it includes all the expectations members have about appropriate attitudes and modes of behavior in your organization. Somewhere spanning all four of those facets is your system of resolving conflicts and maintaining effective internal communications.

Is "High-Performance Teamwork" an Oxymoron?

As organizations move away from hierarchical, disciplined cultures with clear boundaries around function and authority, the management literature encourages their leaders to move them in two contradictory directions. One direction is toward greater *individual responsibility* and *accountability* for performance. The other direction is toward more "systems" concepts such as *learning cultures* and *flexible boundary management*. Those directions are opposite to one another in that the first promotes more competition among individuals to prove their worth to the organization, whereas the second emphasizes more trust and focuses accountability more on the team than the individual. So the experts seem to be pointing toward guaranteed conflict.

The challenge of organizational leadership today is to set a balanced course, capturing the advantages while minimizing the disadvantages of both those trends (and not to completely abandon the control advantages of the old-fashioned hierarchical culture, either). But the right balance for each company depends upon its leaders' analysis of their business, their shared vision, and their long-term goals and strategies.

Imagine a triangle each of whose corners is a terrible way to organize employees (Figure 7-2). At one corner is the extremely hierarchical, well-trained, and disciplined military organization whose troops stand at attention in the tropical sun until they drop. When one soldier collapses, the others stay at attention, eyes straight ahead.

Label that corner Maximum Control.

Figure 7-2. Finding the balance point.

MAXIMUM CONTROL

Military

Most large com-panies

Paternal-istic family business

Olympic gymnastic "team"

Academic institutions

Many American families

MAXIMUM INTERNAL COMPETITION

MAXIMUM TRUST AND INTERNAL SUPPORT

Another corner is individualism: each man or woman an island, all relationships competitive, self-serving, and transitory, everyone out for the almighty Self. Think of an advertising agency or law firm where every partner is a prima donna, or consider an Olympic gymnastic "team." American society was founded, in part, on the myth of individualism, which can sometimes go too far. Business organizations are often viewed as anti-individualist, but some widespread practices fall near the "everyone out for themselves" corner: the use of temporary workers as commodity labor, for example, or the management style of pitting one's subordinates against each other in a battle for favor and survival.

Label that corner Maximum Internal Competition.

The model for the third corner is a mutually supportive family—not necessarily well functioning, but with a high degree of trust in one another's loyalty. Habitually enmeshed in one another's affairs, their behavior couldn't be more different from the soldiers at attention. When one member sneezes, business stops while everyone hands him a tissue.

Label that corner Maximum Trust and Internal Support.
(Of course, this doesn't mean their efforts are necessarily effective or even constructive.)

Those three models merely anchor the triangle. Your company is somewhere inside that space. Where is it actually?
Where should it be ideally?

The Maximum Control corner, though historically effective
in winning wars, is certainly not what management experts
and business leaders advocate today. As they emphasize group
learning, team building, communications, flexible boundary
management, and participative cultural change, they challenge
managers to move away from the military model toward—
what? Increasing demands for accountability, performance-
based compensation and incentives, and a tone of intense
competitiveness (internal as well as external) suggest the indi-
vidualist corner.

At the same time, the current literature is full of two hot ideas
from social systems theory that seem to suggest enmeshment:
the boundaryless organization and the learning organization.
With the phrase *team building* as popular today as *family values*,
individualism looks like the wave of the past. What are the im-
plications of more lateral communications; overlapping func-
tions; shared initiatives, decisions, and accountability? Should
a business be "one big family" after all?

The new literature says yes, in a way: Greater consciousness
of organizations as systems and better use of the learning
power of teams *must* mean acquiring the ability to manage people who have powerful and emotionally significant relationships with one another. Does that mean stocking up on tis-
sues? No. No one suggests that the corner zone is desirable.
We're not talking about going so far as to take on the *problems*
of family life.

Or are we?

The new organization requires managers and their subordinates to live without the clear boundaries of hierarchy, function, and geography they knew in the past. In place of those
come invisible, flexible, permeable boundaries, described in a
Harvard Business Review article as ". . . more psychological than

organizational. They aren't drawn on a company's organizational chart but in the minds of its managers and employees. . . . Knowing how to recognize these new boundaries and use them productively is the essence of management in the flexible organization."[1] The only guideposts through that hyperspace, the authors tell us, are managers' "own gut feelings about work and the people with whom they do it."

That is terrifying. It means more uncertainty, much more risk of conflict. Live with it, say the experts.

Then along comes another group of experts writing about "the learning organization."[2] Put aside the leader's vision, transmitted down through the ranks. The truly visionary leader is one who understands the limits of his or her own vision well enough to empower others to perpetually create, question, and renew their shared understanding of what their changing environment demands of them.

> Organizations need to become ever more capable of learning how to work ever more interdependently on projects they must constantly redesign.

Although educational philosopher John Dewey stressed the same point nearly one hundred years ago, it is only the recent spread of systems thinking that has brought the learning philosophy into management theory, into the annual reports and speeches of CEOs around the world, into the practices of succession planning consultants. We cannot select the next generation of leaders on the basis of what they already know how to do. We cannot even select them for what they are capable of learning. We need managers who can lead their teams and their organizations *to become ever more capable of learning how to work ever more interdependently on projects they must constantly redesign.*

Terrifying. Exciting, yes, and challenging, but the greater potential for conflicts is obvious. The "learning culture" is as full of uncertainty and risk as is the "boundaryless organization."

Boundary Management

Many factors in today's business environment dictate less bureaucratic, more flexible, team-oriented management. The days are past when you could minimize conflict by minimizing contact; that is, by erecting organizational boundaries.

On the other hand, you can't simply throw out all distinctions of authority, function, reference group, and knowledge. Nor do you want to eliminate all competition among units within the organization; only the wasteful or destructive infighting. Boundaries will still exist, but now managers must artfully balance the efficiency of autonomous teams with the informational power of networks.

This problem of managing boundaries flexibly is inseparable from the problem of interpersonal conflict in organizations. Conflict may be a result of inadequate boundaries, but it can also lead to dysfunctionally rigid ones. Put another way, "good fences make good neighbors" but bad neighbors sometimes erect walls. So the best dispute resolution is really maintenance work on those fences and on the stiles that allow human beings but not beasts to cross them. It goes a long way toward creating a healthy balance between structure and flexibility.

Controlling the Costs and Risks of a Performance Culture vs. a Learning Culture

One of the advantages of CRS is that it is just as much a means of reducing excessive loyalty and enmeshment (avoiding the lower right corner of Figure 7-2) as it is a means of reducing excessive conflict and internal competition (avoiding the lower left corner). All of the systematic sequence of interventions, from goal sorting to active listening, to clarifying and valuing differences, to analyzing the problem maintenance cycle, are aimed at bringing the team back to a balanced course.

The hot concepts "flexible boundaries" and "learning cultures" are both trends away from unrealistic attempts to over-organize and overcontrol from the top. The question is how *far* to move in that direction without losing individual accountability for contributing to profitability.

> True high performance isn't an extreme, it's a balance.

If corporations advocate more flexibility in people's roles, more openness to change, and more trust in teams to redefine their tasks constantly, they must plan how to get the high performance teamwork without the excessive internal competition and potentially destructive conflict. The best team building doesn't produce conflict-free teamwork. The team will constantly benefit from, and transcend, conflict. Ideally, the team undergoes a learning curve in its ability to resolve conflicting ideas and approaches.

The need to reward high-performing individuals and replace underperformers might appear compatible with the idea of teams. Simply shift the performance criteria from individual to group performance objectives and compose the teams of high achievers in the first place. But upon deeper reflection, and in practice, there are at least two problems with that solution. One is that individuals with a track record of outstanding achievement, in organizations or in roles that don't require much teamwork, don't always make outstanding team members. The other problem is that even talented and motivated people take *time to learn* to communicate well and to facilitate one another's performance. An organizational culture with low tolerance for the gradual pace of human development will tend to keep changing the players and thus may never achieve the level of teamwork they are capable of.

When I explained to the human resources vice president of a large public company how its contentious division presidents were like feuding siblings in a family business, he quickly pointed out, "But we're not a family. Our culture emphasizes that if the linebacker isn't doing his job, he's off the team and we'll get a new linebacker." He didn't think a knowledge of social systems based on the dynamics of families would apply to teams of unrelated individuals. My reply, and the conclusion of this book, is that an effective team combines *both* the best features of successful families and the carrot-and-stick (or, to be precise, the carrot-and-ax) accountability found in any competitive business. It's a balancing act.

The culture of teamwork takes a more sophisticated view of "nonperformance" and encourages shared responsibility for turning it around (up to a point, of course).

> Teamwork isn't an extreme. It, too, is a balance.

It does not mean "all for one and one for all." It means taking advantage of the ability to communicate laterally, changing functional roles as situations require, sharing responsibility and accountability. However, at the same time, it can hold individuals even more responsible for facilitating the group's mission, and even more accountable to one another and the organization, than in a hierarchical culture with functional autonomy (which suffers from the "Not my job" syndrome).

Making CRS a Big Deal

Let's assume you decide to launch a program specifically under a name like CRS. What you call it is not important. A company called Telebux might launch TACT, the Telebux Anti-Conflict Teamwork program; one called Kaiser, KCRS, the Kaiser Conflict-Resolving System; and so on. The only point of giving it a name and acronym or abbreviation is to call attention to your program to leverage it for maximum possible benefit.

More important than what you call it are the following points:

❑ *All disputes are now constructively resolvable.* Make it clear to everyone in the organization that you now have *systematic* conflict resolution procedures. Disputes aren't left to chance, or to the catch-as-catch-can skills and institutions that individual managers happen to have acquired in the course of their personal growth.

❑ *Who owns the changes?* If and when CRS becomes part of your organization's culture, it will be because of many people's efforts in formal meetings and informal discussions over a period of months. It's important that the leaders—bosses, group leaders, or consultants—shouldn't take much credit for the change. If it happened, it happened because of the participants themselves; and making that loud and clear is much more than just a courtesy. It's absolutely essential for the members themselves to know they were the ones who solved the problem. They should be proud of having achieved it, rather than viewing it as something done to them. Why? Because they must believe *they can* apply the same skills to other conflicts in the future.

❑ *Publicizing CRS as a permanent asset.* When you go beyond trying to resolve a particular issue and introduce a formal program to bring this system to your organization, the news belongs in your company's newsletter and on plaques on people's walls. If you hold a retreat to work on these matters, you might commemorate it with a suitable embossed gift for each participant. The point of all such gestures is to keep reiterating that CRS is one attribute of our identity as an organization of which we are deservedly proud.

❑ *Extending the system.* We have stressed that within-organization disputes are fundamentally different from disputes between unrelated parties. But where is the boundary around your "organization"? Your enterprise as a whole involves customers, vendors (including consultants), shareholders, lenders, government. Hence a "within-organization" problem-solving system extends to relationships with those who formerly might have been considered "others." In the same way that quality control is part of alliance building with your extended enterprise partners, CRS is a key asset in your strategic alliances and in gaining and holding competitive advantage.

Conclusions: The Challenge of Working Together

As a way of organizing your methods for resolving disputes and facilitating teamwork, anyone who has team-building responsibilities can use systematic conflict resolution. However, for it to play a supporting role in the greater system—the organizational culture—depends upon some prior steps.

The challenge of organizational leadership today is to set a balanced course between competitive elements of culture such as performance reviews and accountability, and trust-based elements such as boundary spanning and the learning organization. Teamwork and high performance both demand that balance, so the idea of "high-performance teamwork" is not an oxymoron. However, the location of the best balance for a particular organization—how much control, how much emphasis on performance, how much trust and support for people—will depend on that organization's long-term goals and strategies.

The culture of teamwork takes a sophisticated view of "nonperformance," recognizes that talented and motivated people *take time to learn* to work together, and encourages shared responsibility for that learning. Hence CRS is an indispensable tool for the organization whose leaders determine to find and maintain their optimal balance between internal competition and cooperation. However, for this to be useful as a whole system, as part of the organization's culture, the strategic plan must have addressed not just markets, products, finance, and growth questions, but also questions about how people are going to work together. To what extent will their performance evaluations reflect teamwork? Are the teams themselves, the actual working groups and cross-function planning groups, in competition with one another within the company as a whole? Or is the organization itself a team of teams?

Although the answers to such questions are beyond the domain of this book, you will need to address them *prior* to the question of whether CRS should be an explicit part of your culture.

Consultants can guide the learning culture, the boundary-permeating process, and the transition to new leadership, but they can never be the *source* of any of those three things. The culture itself must support a commitment to learning and a balance between functional responsibilities and open communication. That happens only in an organization whose leaders actively commit themselves to it.

Notes

1. Larry Hirschhorn and Thomas Gilmore, "The New Boundaries of the 'Boundaryless' Company," *Harvard Business Review*, May–June 1992 (Vol. 70, No. 3), pp. 104–115.
2. Peter Senge, *The Fifth Discipline* (New York: Doubleday, 1991); D. N. Michael, *On Learning to Plan—And Planning to Learn* (San Francisco: Jossey-Bass, 1985); Edgar Schein, *Organizational Culture and Leadership,* 2d ed. (San Francisco: Jossey-Bass, 1992).

8

Summary:
The System Applied

This chapter has two purposes: to summarize the system for interpersonal problem solving and to provide a reference guide for applying the system to specific problems.

Figure 1-1, the flowchart I introduced in Chapter 1 as a map of the book, is now a set of rules of engagement to carry in your head when you march into the battle. Plans A, B, C, D, and E compose a logical sequence:

Agreement and shared goals: Focus on these first, and keep coming back to them.

But, we still have differences. Clarify them, value them, sort out those that you can eliminate in various ways.

Commit people to change.

Diagram the chronic cycle of sustained conflict. Have they been fighting together to avoid talking about important issues?

Excel, personally: If others won't budge, what can you do unilaterally?

This sequence begins with the simplest approach to a win/win resolution, then adds more-challenging approaches—only as they are needed (Figure 1-1). But there is nothing rigid about that sequence, no limit to the number of times you might return to an approach either before or after moving on. My mentor in systematic conflict resolution, Professor William Pinsof, used to compare it to the art of a jazz musician—learning and practicing the scales, chords, and riffs so well that one can improvise on them, never using them quite the same way. No two performances of our chart with different ensembles will be alike, but all will involve the musical elements of discord, tension, and harmonic resolution.

Before showing how you might perform all that jazz in a variety of cases, let me reprise what I said in Chapter 1 about *when* to use the techniques in this book.

There are two fundamentally different kinds of dispute resolution. We hear and read more about the external kind, between people who will have an arms-length relationship, at best, after their settlement. That would include disputes between unrelated or divorcing individuals or between permanent adversary groups, such as unions and management with their opposing battalions of attorneys. Conflict resolution *within* a family or working group gets much less attention in the press as well as the professional literature, even though it is part of our lives every day.

Although this book is concerned with the latter, the within-group kind, you may have noticed that some of the observations and suggestions in Chapters 2 and 3 apply to either kind of conflict. For example, an attorney negotiating a settlement for her client in a tort matter or a contract dispute would look for the win/win solution by concentrating on shared goals, clearing up any misunderstandings between the two sides, and clarifying their differences. She would also employ active listening and positive reframing. So would a neutral mediator in such disputes. In addition, though, the negotiator for one side might use threats and ultimatums, which aren't appropriate in situations where the parties need to have a relationship afterward. Because they are based on power rather than trust, such tactics for controlling others are of little use to the leaders of an organization that is experiencing internal conflict.

This system as a whole is specifically designed for any and all disputes between persons who cannot or will not walk out of each other's lives. Notwithstanding their human emotions, neuroses, personality differences, and cultural diversity, they need to work together. They don't have to be friends, but they do need to be teammates. And the person who employs this system is neither a hired gun for one side nor a neutral, but a change agent (a leader in the best sense of the word) helping them build more effective communications and more constructive relationships.

Case Applications

We conclude with a sampling of such situations. Some are similar to examples in earlier chapters, but the purpose here is to follow the overview, the flow through different approaches as needed.The CRS flowchart (Figure 1-1) adapts to virtually any conflict within a group or organization, with contingencies for the most cooperative types of people as well as the least cooperative. Test your understanding of the brief rationale for applying it to each of these cases or just flip to whichever case rings the most bells for you.

Disaffected Partners

You and a friend started a business with $20,000 and no employees. After eight years, you have sixty employees, 30 percent annual growth, and a mutual frustration that keeps you avoiding one another for days at a time and threatens to tear your business apart. You don't trust one another's judgment, perhaps; or one another's commitment, or people skills. Of course, you resent your partner's disaffection and you miss the friendship.

This is a case for outside help. As one of the antagonists, you can't be the mediator. Nor can you put any of your employees or either of your spouses in that position.

Plan A asks whether you both want to maintain this business partnership. If either owner has already decided to end it, then it becomes a question of whether one buys the other out or you both sell the whole company. It turns out, however, that your partner adamantly wants to stay in the business. His first preference would be to restore a constructive co-ownership; failing that, to buy you out. You share the same first preference, but not the second. You don't care to analyze all the alternative options unless they become necessary, but for a variety of reasons you'd have grave reservations about selling your half to him.

That issue can be set aside while addressing the shared goal of working constructively together if possible. You spell out what that means to each of you, in terms of business goals, division of responsibilities, and the personal relationship. You find you still have a common vision for the business. With respect to the friendship, though, your partner doesn't acknowledge sharing your feelings. "We're not the same people we were ten or fifteen years ago," he says. "Our personal lives have gone in very different directions." You decide, pragmatically, to give up hoping to resuscitate the friendship outside of work.

Remaining on the table are all the issues about who is responsible for what: how best to pursue your vision as owners and as a president and a chief financial officer. The differences in your analysis of what specifically has been destructive in the past (who is to blame for what) are so extensive that merely reaffirming your shared goal and brainstorming together about how to achieve it don't get you anywhere.

Your facilitator suggests Plan B. After clearing away a couple of misunderstandings, you focus upon the complementary strengths that led you to value each other's business partnership originally. Hearing your partner say that the company would never have enjoyed such success had it not been for your talents and vision (something you're not sure you ever heard him say before) has a significant effect upon your attitude. You give him credit for a number of specific things that he has done excellently. The problem is that numerous minor aggravations, which he dismisses as unimportant, have built a huge reservoir of resentment on your part and led him to feel that you don't trust him.

The question becomes, then, what needs to change? An hour and a half into your first conflict-resolution meeting, you reach Plan C. That turns out to be as far as you need go. Although you meet with your consultant half a dozen times over the next year, the agenda is essentially the same: to review the commitments each of you made, assess your changes, and go back through Plans A and B with respect to current issues and the status of old issues.

The heart of this successful resolution was Plan B, restoring the value of your different styles and talents. Plan A established the reason for doing so. Plan C spelled out the specific behavior you asked of one another and the specific changes you agreed to. Was there no sustained conflict cycle that could have been analyzed insightfully? There almost certainly was, and getting into Plan D might be a stimulating exercise in understanding interpersonal dynamics. But you don't need to do so as long as you and your partner are really ending your feud. Plan B does the trick.

Uncomplementary Teammates

Suppose you are director of human resources and training for a medium-size advertising agency whose creative talent look contemptuously at the account executives, treating their input as stupid meddling. The account executives and staff retaliate by criticizing the creative work and failing to show enthusiasm for it in the presence of clients. Accusations of sexual discrimination only exacerbate the lack of teamwork. Your boss, the agency's president, doesn't see how she has contributed to the problem.

You design a series of retreats to gain the whole agency's involvement in attitude change and better teamwork. The first meeting is to include the president, heads of creative and account services, and the twelve group directors. (All of the firm's accounts and the employees who serve them directly are assigned to groups. Later, you plan to hold "grass-roots" retreats for one to three groups, about fifteen people, at a time; but only after the group creative directors and group account directors—and most importantly, the president—buy in to the project.)

To prepare for the first retreat, you interview each participant individually. Partly your goals are to learn in advance what axes they are grinding and to be sure your agenda and format will meet their goals. Equally important, you walk each group director through a structured questionnaire, which they are to use in meeting with their groups prior to your retreat. These questions will increase the possibility that group directors' views reflect those of their teams.

Your interviews make it clear that everyone at least claims the same goal: "to do outstanding, memorable creative work that exceeds clients' objectives and makes a profit for our agency." Therefore, you decide there's no need to dwell on Plan A at the outset.

As in the foregoing example, Plan B is the heart of this case: valuing the different perspectives of the account executives versus the creatives. But giving lip service to the ways they *should* complement one another is trivial. The challenge is to train both types to discuss their point-of-view differences as they arise—and will continue to arise in the future—in the heat of specific battles.

Thus the first retreat is virtually all Plan B. You don't concern yourself with committing individuals to change their behavior. Nor do you attack directly, at this stage, the president's resistance. The only behavior change you will push for, throughout the day, is active listening. You keep asking, "How can we do a better job of listening to one another, of getting the information we need from one another, of getting our ideas and our needs across to one another, and thereby trusting each other to meet our clients' needs?" And you show them how.

Plan C will come later, with these same people as well as at the level of the creative directors, writers, artists, and account executives. When people persist in feeling (as they will) that one another's habitual behavior is an obstacle to their teamwork, then you will use Plan C to deflect the finger pointing and to target changes for each individual.

The first meeting is a success. The president is praised for authorizing and convening it. Two months later, after five comparable retreats in which the creative teams serving a particular group of clients meet with the corresponding account executives, you reconvene with top management. Sliding into Plan C, you do the finger trap exercise (Figure 4-1). And the top row and first column are labeled with the president's name.

Does this lead to a breakthrough? Probably only a partial

breakthrough. You are "joining," bonding with each individual, validating appropriate parts of all parties' positions. And you are using those alliances to push for change. As it becomes clearer how much the president has contributed to the problem and how much more she must contribute to the solution, you meet more frequently with her, one to one. You offer to sit in on some of her meetings with the head of creative and the head of client services.

You wait. The occasion for Plan D may come when you have accomplished two things:

1. You have won the top managers' trust. They believe that what you are doing is important.
2. A crisis occurs—a serious conflict arises and escalates, leading people to groan, "Here we go again"—and they believe that you can be helpful.

Until such an event occurs, you keep the shared purposes of everyone in the organization at the forefront of their minds, and you keep using Plans B and C to improve their efforts toward those ends.

Relative in the Family Business

You are an outside consultant to the owner of a manufacturing firm who has five adult children. The business could easily employ the talents of all three who are interested, except for the fact that the oldest son and daughter have no respect for their kid brother. He accepts no responsibility, they say; he holds himself accountable to no one, bends Dad around his little finger and acts like he's entitled to the same rewards as they. Kid brother complains that they give him no authority, reject his ideas out of hand, and exclude him from meetings. Dad claims he could "sell the whole damn business" without hesitation; but his heart is breaking.

Although the company is your client, keep in mind that you have at least three other individuals with whom you need alliances, in addition to those who work there: the owner's wife and their other two offspring. Don't neglect his daughters- and sons-in-law, either, all of whom have a significant stake in (and strong opinions about) the company's future ownership, and some of whom may be central figures in the conflict.

However, after an initial meeting with the three who work in the business, you decide to hold a series of two- to three-hour meetings in your own office with just them and their father. Prior to the first of those meetings, you interview their mother and the spouses of those who are married, but by mutual agreement, they won't be in the first series of meetings. You term these meetings "family management sessions." A full "family retreat," which will also include the other two siblings and spouses, is planned for later.

In the first session, Plan A seems to go well, with everyone apparently in agreement about their goals for the business as well as for their family relationships. From your private interviews, you know that the players in this drama have many conflicting individual goals. Surprisingly, though, you find them reluctant to express openly their fundamentally different objectives, bitter resentments, and distrust. So you raise the issues they avoid. When you do so, Plan B gets nowhere. Everyone is rigidly defensive and accusatory. In Plan C, they are full of demands for one another to change; each individual, including Dad, has airtight excuses not to change.

You begin to ask about patterns of conflict. As an investigator in the style of Peter Falk's television detective Columbo, you ask nonaccusatory questions about what typically leads to what. What might happen if the kid brother were performing better? What if they did treat him as an equal? What if they didn't have that issue to fight about?

In the course of continued discussion of specific complaints and confrontations over several more sessions, this line of questioning (Plan D) gives you insight about the conflict, which you share with the members. You see a softening of the older brother's and sister's positions, but their father's impatience increases. When you return to Plan C, he doesn't acknowledge a need or willingness to change his management style or his way of relating to any of them. Worse, the youngest son makes all the right verbal commitments but doesn't execute them: He continues to arrive late, leave early, take employees out for long lunches, ignore deadlines. He continues to mismanage his personal finances and to use his company credit card as a slush fund.

Before the family retreat, you meet separately with the parents and encourage them to stop enabling their son's failures. You also support the older siblings' independent, unilateral actions to protect the business. You try to gain their commitment to cease blaming each other while maintaining the problem. Although not unsympathetic to the kid brother, you encourage him to think seriously about other possible careers. All these are efforts to sell Plan E, unilateral change, to whoever will buy it.

Eventually, the youngest brother will leave the business, perhaps to return after he has matured outside the protective umbrella of his family. Meanwhile, you have established a long-term advisory relationship with the whole family, which will culminate five to ten years later in a successful transition to next generation ownership.

Excessive, Unproductive Competition Between Divisions

You are CEO of a fairly large corporation consisting of two divisions. Alpha Division manufactures a building product; Beta Division wholesales and retails throughout North America several lines of building material, including that of Alpha Division, of which it is the largest customer. You wouldn't mind a friendly rivalry between the two divisions, competing to exceed their targets and dazzle the shareholders, but for some reason they treat each other like enemies. The heads of the two divisions openly dislike one another, trading accusations about matters as significant as fraudulent accounting practices and as trivial as the allocation of parking spaces. Alpha Division's president seems to be able to control his violent temper just enough to aim it selectively in the direction of Beta Division's managers. The two presidents ought to be collaborating on a number of fronts, because their divisions aren't really divisible. In fact, in some locations many of your employees split their time between the two divisions during at least part of the year. That invariably provokes disputes over cost allocations, reporting relationships, and responsibilities. Morale in both divisions is in the subbasement.

You call both presidents in and announce that you have already made a nonnegotiable decision. It is both their responsibilities—and a top priority—to ensure that their divisions collaborate positively with one another. You will tolerate no excuses for their failure to turn the situation around, least of all excuses that blame one another. What you have done, effectively, is to combine Plan A with Plan E: You have unilaterally decreed their shared goal.

At the same time, you tell them that you take full responsibility for having contributed to the problem in the past, partly by allowing it to deteriorate but probably also in more direct ways, which you want to explore, and that you want to know what they need you to do differently. You are anticipating Plan C, at least to set the stage for a commitment to change and to provide a model of asking what each president can change. You may even spend some time on their preliminary ideas about changes. However, you will return to Plan C in earnest after Plan B.

Plan B will involve others in the company, as well as the three of you. You may or may not attend all of their meetings on the two divisions' different objectives, incentives, and perspectives. They may want someone else to facilitate those meetings, or they may want to cochair them. All this is open to discussion; in fact, the project of analyzing and making joint recommendations about those differences will itself be the first example of the new spirit of cooperation you are demanding.

Let us envision two alternative, equally likely scenarios over the next six to twelve months. In one, the president of either Alpha or Beta Division resigns. Is that good? Yes, because chances are, it's the better person who will stay. The previous state of affairs would have led the better person to leave. You have created pressure for collaboration rather than destructiveness; the first to leave under these conditions is probably the one you are well rid of.

But there is another scenario, just as frequent in my experience. The problem diminishes, gradually but significantly. The foregoing steps will not be sufficient to bring that about. You'll need to use Plan D when the changes made so far prove inadequate or when the managers backslide into habitual battles: Look for the common pattern in those battles, and then use the information gained from all such discussions (Plans B and D) to pinpoint further specific changes (down to the details of how the accountants allocate individual employees' wages, insurance, workers compensation, etc., to the two divisions).

Notice that despite all the pressure you put on your subordinates to correct the problem, in the final analysis Plan E will play a big role in the solution. The buck stops with you.

Isolated Explosion

Your company president calls you in to resolve "some sort of hen fight" between his 26-year-old secretary and the 58-year-old secretary to the chairman. The two women's desks are within spitting distance, but they have worked well together for three years, covering each other's telephones and days off. Both are valued employees. You find the younger woman in tears, hurt by her mentor's far-fetched accusations about a conspiracy to make her look bad by deprogramming her voice mail and sabotaging computer files. Other employees report that the senior secretary had been screaming profanity at her junior—language they wouldn't have thought was in her vocabulary. They feel sure there must have been some provocation.

You may get this call because you are the company's personnel director, another key executive known for your sensitivity and people skills, or perhaps the company's attorney. In any case, before sitting down with the two employees, you interview them separately to try to learn what happened. The possibility exists that the outburst was a manifestation of some chronic problem involving their bosses (the president's unsympathetic, sexist remark about the "hen fight" could be a clue), but as you compare what they say, you realize that you are deep in the "individual issues" section of Plan B.

The younger woman, though upset and embarrassed,

gives a consistent and plausible account of what she experienced, and her hurt feelings seem entirely appropriate to the circumstances. Furthermore, she is concerned about the other woman. She acknowledges the possibility that she may actually have offended her. She welcomes your help in doing whatever she can to make amends.

The other woman seems, in laymen's terms, crazy. She is absolutely convinced that she is the victim of a conspiracy, tells you that she knows you are biased in favor of the younger woman, expects to be fired, and has already put in a call to her lawyer.

You are neither a detective nor a psychiatrist, but this employee seems to have a mental health problem of unknown origin. (It could be anything from a brain tumor, to a side effect of medication, to emotional stress at home.) Because she has no history of paranoia, the chances are quite good that she will respond well to professional treatment. However, she has to be forced to seek or accept treatment, and any pressure in that direction, unfortunately, will intensify her symptom.

You advise the company's chairman personally to tell his secretary that she is a valued employee but that something has happened to her which makes her temporarily unable to perform her job. He can hold the job open for her a couple of weeks in case, with her doctor's help, she gets to the root of the problem quickly. If she is unable to return to work in the near future, every effort will be made to find a place for her in the company at some future date. Alternatively, she can accept a severance package more generous than a secretary would normally receive.

I include this case as a reminder that not every conflict resolves as happily as we might like. In fact, this employee threatens to sue the company. However, the attorney she retains, a friend of her brother, learns from the company's counsel what occurred, how all steps have been documented, and how well she is being treated. He, too, becomes convinced something is wrong with his client and suggests to her family that she be assessed psychiatrically. Some months later, she accepts the severance offer.

Culture Change?

Each example is an actual one from among my clients. In each case, I tried to do more than help resolve the specific issue of the moment. As explained in Chapter 7, I always look for opportunities to leverage the specific dispute resolution into an openly proclaimed culture change with visible, sustainable effects on the company's productivity. In how many of these cases did that happen? In two cases that kind of culture change definitely occurred (the advertising agency and the company with competing divisions). In a third case, the disaffected partners have moved so far in the direction of better teamwork that their culture as a whole is changing slowly, as a result. In the other two cases, there was no evidence of any organizational improvement beyond the benefits of having resolved the problem at hand.

But that itself is no small achievement.

Appendix:
Active Listening

Whether one is a manager or supervisee, teacher or learner, salesperson or customer, parent or child, friend, or spouse, the goals of active listening are the same:

- ❏ To understand clearly what other people are saying, including the motives and feelings behind their words
- ❏ To make them feel they have been fully heard and clearly understood
- ❏ To make them feel that whether you agree with them or not, you respect their point of view
- ❏ To increase the likelihood that they will follow these same goals with you, in return

In the course of daily life, good communicators use active listening skills informally and unobtrusively. The best way to learn them, however, is in a strict, formal routine. Later, you will only resort to that formal (and slightly artificial) routine in circumstances of great stress or volatility. But when training yourself or training others, enforce the rules of active listening strictly.

Normally you'll only think of introducing those rules when a heated argument gets out of hand because of the *lack* of active listening. For example, Hank and Russ are business partners, cofounders of a transportation company with seventy-five employees in six different offices:

Dialogue I

Hank: When I got the call from Ray in Milwaukee, I knew before he told me why he was calling. I said to myself, "Russ has done it again!" I knew he was going to tell me you tried to convince him he didn't need the computer.

Russ: I didn't try to convince him of anything.

Hank: Like hell you didn't. You called him up. I didn't ask you to call him. I said, "Ray needs one of the new computers. Add one to the order and have it shipped directly to him." Period. End of discussion.

Russ: That was no discussion, that was a voice mail message. I can never get you to discuss anything, so I simply called Ray for clarification.

Hank: No, you called Ray for confusion. Does Ray report to you?

Russ: What difference does it make who he . . .

Hank [louder]: Does Ray report to you?

Russ [equally louder]: What difference does it make who he reports to? I'm in charge of purchasing, and . . .

Hank: So *purchase*! I didn't tell you to find out if he really needed a computer, and I certainly didn't tell you to try to convince him he could get along without it after I told him otherwise.

Russ [sarcastically]: Why don't I purchase *sixty* computers? We have seventy-five employees and only fifteen computers. Why don't we get . . .

Hank: Good. Now we're getting to the real issue. In other words, you hear me mention the word *buy* and it scares the pants off you. Right away your sirens go off and I'm bankrupting the company.

Russ: Why do you take everything so personally? I didn't say you were bankrupting the company. You've tried a few times, but you haven't succeeded yet. It's my job to . . .

Hank [yelling at the top of his voice, turning red]: Listen, you so-and-so, I have grown this company by 40 percent or more every year of the six years we have been in business, and I have had to fight you for every pencil to take an order with.

Russ [calmly]: You know what, Hank?

Hank [on a roll]: I couldn't get a decent chair for a visitor to sit on in my office; you tried to bring in one out of your great-grandmother's garage . . .

Russ [*louder*]: You know what, Hank? I've had it. I'm through with this. This partnership is over. If I have to go on, time and again, defending myself for introducing reality into your fantasy world . . .

We won't attempt here to discuss the merits of Hank's and Russ's complaints about one another, because they aren't giving the merits of their arguments a chance. The fact that they aren't listening to one another eliminates any possibility of escaping the vicious circle of their mutually distrustful relationship. It isn't hard to see where they go wrong:

- ❑ By interrupting each other, neither person ever gets the satisfaction of being heard.
- ❑ By losing track of who has the floor, they aren't even aware of who interrupted whom.
- ❑ By jumping in with rebuttals and accusations, they guarantee that the temperature will rise until the confrontation ends either in violence or the threat to dissolve the partnership.

Active listening prevents all that. It does not guarantee that the partners will decide to stay in business together. In fact, it doesn't prevent them from maintaining the same cycle of sustained conflict (the subject of Chapter 5), but it is the necessary first step if they are ever to break out of that cycle. It guarantees that they won't keep escalating the conflict to the point where it is all heat and no light.

The rules for active listening are simple:

Rules for the Speaker

- ❑ Must not yield the floor until (s)he feels listened to.
- ❑ Should not ask a question until (s)he is prepared to switch roles and listen to the answer.

Rules for Listeners

- ❑ Must not reply, express any opinion, or signal disagreement with any of speaker's statements.

❏ Must reflect back what they understand to be speaker's views (acknowledging and verifying the negative or disagreeable views as well as the positive).
❏ Must ask questions to clarify anything they don't understand.
❏ When they want to reply, must first check to be sure they have understood correctly and then get permission to be the new speaker.

Clearly, the key to active listening is for all parties in the conversation to know, at all times, who has the floor. The rules for whoever has the floor, the speaker, are different from the rules for everyone else, the listeners. The listeners aren't silent; in fact, they are active interviewers but are restricted to asking questions and checking their own understanding.

A listener has to request permission to take the floor; the speaker only consents when he is sure he has been heard.

So the discussion between Hank and Russ would go something like this:

Dialogue II

Hank [*speaker*]: When I got the call from Ray in Milwaukee, I knew before he told me why he was calling. I said to myself, "Russ has done it again!" I knew he was going to tell me you tried to convince him he didn't need the computer.

Russ [*listener*]: Is that what he said?

Hank [*speaker*]: You called him up—and I didn't ask you to call him. I said, "Ray needs one of the new computers. Add one to the order and have it shipped directly to him." Period. End of discussion.

Russ [*listener*]: So your view is that you gave me an instruction and I failed to carry it out.

Hank [*speaker*]: That's correct.

Russ [*listener*]: And it really pissed you off.

Hank [*speaker*]: Yes, as it always does.

Russ [*listener*]: May I respond to that?

Hank [*becoming listener, though dubious*]: I would like to hear your response.

Russ [*speaker*]: As a matter of fact, I do accept that whether Ray gets a computer is your decision. If I had been sure you weighed all the factors and decided we should go ahead and add one more computer to the current purchase order, then so be it. But all I got was one sentence on my voice mail. I then left a message for you and when you didn't get back to me, I figured you wouldn't want me to do nothing at all about it until whenever, so I took it upon myself to make sure you had asked Ray all the pertinent questions.

Hank [*out of order*]: That's just it! You . . .

Russ [*speaker*]: Just a minute, I have the floor. My problem is I can never get you to discuss anything, so I simply called Ray for clarification.

Although the speaker may say whatever he wants, the active listening framework has made it easy for Russ to use additional techniques of constructive dialogue (see Figure 2-2). Thus he acknowledges the part of Hank's position with which he has no quarrel ("I do accept that . . .") and he says "My problem is . . ." instead of "Your fault is. . . ."

Hank [*listener*]: Now may I respond to that?

Russ [*speaker*]: What did you hear me saying?

Hank [*listener*]: That you called Ray for clarification.

Russ [*speaker*]: Because?

Hank [*listener*]: Because you weren't sure I had grilled Ray closely enough on his rationale for needing another computer.

Russ [*speaker*]: Exactly. I felt you had identified a need but you were delegating the purchasing to me—appropriately. And the first step in purchasing is to explore the possibility of making do with what we have.

Hank [*listener*]: So in your mind you weren't questioning my decision; you were merely implementing it in your own fashion.

Russ [*speaker*]: If you want to put it that way.

Hank [*becoming the speaker*]: Now, my turn? I didn't tell you to find out if he really needed a computer, and I certainly didn't tell you to try to convince him he could get along without it after I told him otherwise.

Russ [*listener*]: Is that what you think I did?

Hank [*speaker*]: That is exactly what I think you did. Didn't you?

Now Russ may resume the floor, because Hank has just asked a question.

Russ [*speaker*]: No, I don't believe I did. Maybe he interpreted . my questions as trying to talk him out of his position, but that's not what I intended.

Hank [*listener*]: What, pray tell, did you intend?

Russ [*speaker*]: Only to be sure that the questions had been asked and answered to my satisfaction. If I'd had a chance to talk with you directly instead of trading voice mail messages, I would have asked you if you had already had that discussion with Ray. Lacking that opportunity (for which I blame you, frankly), I did the best I could.

Hank [*listener*]: Look, Russ, is that the real issue: that we don't discuss every little decision in detail? Or is it that you hear me mention the word *buy* and it scares the pants off you? Right away your sirens go off and I'm bankrupting the company.

Russ [*treating Hank's out-of-order assertion as a question, thus retaining the floor*]: I didn't say you were bankrupting the company. You've come close a few times, but we're still solvent. It's my job to . . .

In short, the same two frustrated individuals can discuss the same difficult issue without getting out of control.

The best thing about active listening is that you don't have to get the other person's agreement to engage in it. *It only takes one person to insist on active listening.* You take responsibility for showing others that you have heard them before you respond, and you also take responsibility for refusing to give them the floor until they demonstrate that they have heard you. If they don't like that, you won't discuss the matter with them.

The Golden Rule of Active Listening

Listen unto others as you would have them listen unto you; but if *they* don't listen when it's *your* turn, don't talk with them.

The reason Dialogue II worked better than Dialogue I is that Russ carefully laid the groundwork for his own chance to be listened to by making sure Hank felt that his anger was fully heard before Russ attempted to reply. This is easy to do if you keep reminding yourself that a listener may only ask clarifying questions, such as:

"Is that what he said?"
"So your view is . . ."
"Does it feel unfair because . . ."
"Are you saying that . . ."
"If I understand you . . ."

Tom uses the technique in this example:

Tom: Why do you seem so hostile whenever I open my mouth in Monday meetings?
Gina: I seem so hostile because I don't like you.
Tom [actively listening]: What don't you like about me?
Gina [speaker]: It is not you as a person. I mean I'm sure you have many fine qualities, but I don't get a chance to find out what they are because I am so offended by your attitude. Particularly I don't like your attitude about women. You never miss an opportunity to make some kind of dig.
Tom [listener]: Could you give me an example?
Gina [speaker]: An example? Sure, let me see. This morning, Fred started to write on the chart, and the blue marker was out of ink. You said, "Oh, Marilyn's falling down on the job."
Tom [listener]: Um hm.

Gina [*speaker*]: Like it's Marilyn's job to check the markers be-
    fore the meeting. Marilyn's not a secretary, but that's not
    even the point. The truth is, you wouldn't have said it to a
    secretary. You're threatened by the women on this team
    because we *aren't* secretaries; and you're probably not
    aware of it, but you feel compelled to put us in our places.
    You have a problem, Tom.
Tom [*listener*]: Was Marilyn offended?
Gina [*speaker*]: You asked me why *I* seem hostile, so I'm telling
    you that *I* am offended every time you say stuff like that,
    no matter who it's directed at.
Tom [*after a pause*]: Well, as I hear you, you're saying I treat . . .

We don't know whether Tom's active listening will lead to
his consciousness-raising and to a commitment to be more
aware of how his "jokes" insult people. But he is doing everything he can to make Gina perceive him as sincerely interested.

As an active listener, you might catch yourself at first asking pseudoquestions that really express an opinion or imply
disbelief. Hank did this at the end of Dialogue II above, when
he slipped an assertion about Russ's paranoia into a "question"
beginning "Or is it that. . . ." You can usually spot a pseu-
doquestion from the opening words:

Pseudoquestions

"Can you really sit there and tell me . . ."
"Don't you realize that's not the reason . . ."
"Haven't I told you a thousand times that . . ."

Such mistakes will land you back in the kind of shouting
match illustrated in Dialogue I above. When pseudoquestions
come at you while you are the speaker, all you need to do instead of defending against a "listener's" assertion is to say,
"Wait a minute; I have the floor."

What do you do when you have the floor but the other
person seems unable to listen to you without hostility? Pause
for a moment and reflect. Are you being aggressive (attacking)
instead of assertive (expressing your own feelings)? Try again.

You can't learn active listening skills just by reading about them. You learn by trying them. The best way is to have a third party observe your conversation. Have them stop any listener who interrupts, fails to ask questions, or expresses or implies a response out of turn. *Before responding, a listener must check whether the speaker feels understood and is ready to yield the floor.* The purpose of such exercises, of course, is to create new norms that will guide the group's behavior at other times when the intervener isn't present.

Index